❦　*The Languages of Paradise*

The Languages of Paradise

Race, Religion, and Philology in the Nineteenth Century

MAURICE OLENDER

Translated by Arthur Goldhammer

HARVARD UNIVERSITY PRESS

Cambridge, Massachusetts
London, England
1992

First published as *Les langues du paradis: Aryens et Sémites, un couple providentiel,*
© Editions du Seuil, 1989.

Publication of this book has been aided by a grant from the Georges Lurcy
Charitable and Educational Trust.

This book is printed on acid-free paper, and its binding materials have been chosen
for strength and durability.

Library of Congress Cataloging-in-Publication Data
Olender, Maurice.
　　　[Langues du paradis. English]
　　　The languages of Paradise: race, religion, and philology in the nineteenth
century / Maurice Olender ; translated by Arthur Goldhammer.
　　　　　p.　cm.
　　　Translation of: Les langues du paradis.
　　　Includes bibliographical references and index.
　　　ISBN 0-674-51052-6 (acid-free paper)
　　　1. Philology—History—19th century.　2. Language and culture—History—
19th century.　I. Title.
P75.0413　1992
400—dc20　　　　　　　　　　　　　　　　　　　　　91-19996
　　　　　　　　　　　　　　　　　　　　　　　　　　　　CIP

🎋 Contents

❧ Foreword

by Jean-Pierre Vernant

Where was Paradise? In what blessed region of the world did God place the Garden of Eden, and what language did Adam and Eve speak when they lived there? Did the first couple, at the dawn of history, converse in Hebrew, as Saint Augustine quite naturally assumed? Or should we, as Leibniz believed, look for a more primitive idiom, the language of the Scythian continent, supposedly the root of the various languages spoken by the so-called Indo-European peoples and thus, in the eyes of scholars, the original speech of humankind? The language of Paradise—language in its original state, human speech as it emerged from the pure state of language itself, the language of God or of the world, of the nature that God created out of nothing by the power of his Word.

The ancient Greeks, curious as they were, seem never to have wondered what language men spoke in the golden age— in that primordial time when mortals and immortals lived together, feasting at the same table in the joy of everlasting youth, without toil, disease, or suffering and without the need to confront, for better or for worse, that other "race," women. But perhaps the answer seemed so obvious that the question was never raised. The language the men of the golden age spoke was of course the only language truly worthy of the name—Greek—as opposed to the unintelligible stammering of the peoples who, because the sounds they uttered were senseless gibberish, were known as barbarians.

These stories make us smile, as though they came to us from

another age, from the childhood of human thought. The philosophers, linguists, historians, and anthropologists of my generation all begin with a common conviction: in order to do successful research in any field of study, they must abandon nostalgic dreams of a primitive golden age and comforting faith in history's providential purpose. In my younger days, when I assisted my teacher I. Meyerson in the task of editing the *Journal de psychologie* founded by Janet and Dumas, I applied to every article we received a rule that I had made my own, first formulated in Article 2 of the charter of the Société de Linguistique: accept no paper concerning the origins of language. On one side there was serious scientific inquiry into the diversity of human tongues, thought, and civilizations; on the other there were fables about the original language and the ultimate purpose of the human adventure. There seemed to be a sharp and definitive division between the strictly rational approach and the naive fantasies of the mythological imagination.

What was naive, however, was our self-assurance: we had been all too quick to forget that, like Descartes's common sense, nothing is more widely shared than imagination. Maurice Olender's book puts our ideas back in their proper context. Olender has followed, step by step, the founding fathers of such important disciplines as philology and comparative mythology, tracking their digressions, doubts, and errors as well as the successes that led ultimately to the human sciences as we practice them today. Quietly and seemingly without effort, Olender destroys the illusion that science made continuous progress guided solely by the sovereign power of reason, much as the Almighty through divine Providence was once supposed to direct from on high the course of human affairs.

After reading this book, one begins to understand that reason does not exist until human beings attempt to understand some aspect of reality and to apply what they learn. Scientific rationality defines itself as it constructs the subject matter and methodology of each new discipline. In the human sciences, moreover, there is no virgin territory to explore; the fields of investigation are continents mapped by tradition and explored by religious thought. Trails have already been blazed, itineraries set out. Then, too, the problems that arise in any new field of study are always in some sense echoes of current social concerns, questions of identity: society seeks to know its roots in the past, its responsibilities in the present, and its fate in the future.

Twenty-five years ago, when I first attacked the problem of the origins of Greek thought and investigated the conditions under which critical intelligence and positive knowledge could develop, I used the formula "from myth to reason." The problem with this formulation is that it suggests that, in the minds of the pioneering sixth-century B.C.E. Milesian philosophers, the issue was one of a necessary choice between two incompatible mental attitudes. Subsequently, of course, the dividing line between *mythos* and *logos* became much sharper, but in the archaic Greek culture from which the "physicians" of the Miletus school sprang, there was no clear demarcation between reason on the one hand and religion, superstition, and myth on the other. Rationality and traditional beliefs coexisted, at times in conflict but always in one way or another intertwined, in a context that was various, to be sure, yet always integrated, because it was a product of the *polis*. In later centuries one part of this originally integrated whole would impose itself as a model of intelligibility, while another part would be portrayed as an absurd fable; but at this stage the two components still supported each other, by which I mean they were complementary and mutually reinforcing even in their divergence.

To our delight and instruction, Maurice Olender brings to light through his unanachronistic readings of Herder, Renan, Max Müller, Pictet, and Grau this paradox: that the nineteenth century, the heyday of positivism and scientism, also produced, in a field where research was most original and intellectually fruitful, what can only be called a tissue of scholarly myths. These myths were steeped in erudition, informed by profound knowledge of Hebrew and Sanskrit, fortified by comparative study of linguistic data, mythology, and religion, and shaped by the effort to relate linguistic structures, forms of thought, and features of civilization. Yet they were also myths, fantasies of the social imagination, at every level. The comparative philology of the most ancient languages was a quest for origins, an attempt to return to a privileged moment in time when God, man, and natural forces still lived in mutual transparency. This plunge into the distant past in search of "roots" went hand in hand with a never forgotten faith in a meaningful history, whose course, guided by the Providence of the one God, could be understood only in the light of Christian revelation. As scholars established the disciplines of Semitic and Indo-European studies, they also invented the mythical figures of the Hebrew and the Aryan, a providential pair which, by revealing to the people of the Christianized West the secret of their identity, also bestowed upon them the patent of nobility that justified their spiritual, religious, and political domination of the world. The balance was not maintained, however, between the two components of this couple. The Hebrew undeniably had the privilege of monotheism in his favor, but he was self-centered, static, and refractory both to Christian values and to progress in culture and science. The Aryan, on the other hand, was invested with all the noble virtues that direct the dynamic of history: imagination, reason, science, arts, politics.

The Hebrew was troublesome, disturbing, problematic: he stood at the very foundation of the religious tradition with which the scholars in question identified, but he was also alien to that tradition. Wherever he lived, under the name of Jew, in a specific place among a specific people, he remained an outsider, aloof, different. On him, therefore, focused the tensions, repudiations, and hostilities that the image of the Other elicits from individuals as well as nations.

In these two linked but asymmetrical mirror-mirages, these projections in which nineteenth-century scholars attempted to discern their own image, we cannot today fail to see looming in the background the dark silhouette of the death camps and the rising smoke of the ovens.

✿ Preface

I met Georges Dumézil and Léon Poliakov in 1975. Shortly thereafter I read Raymond Schwab's *La renaissance orientale,* published by Payot in 1950. Some of the questions that led me to embark on the historiographical quest whose first stage is described in this book were most certainly the result of this triple encounter.

The chapters of this book took shape in connection with seminars that I have given in recent years. In 1985, François Furet, then president of the Ecole des Hautes Etudes en Sciences Sociales, asked me to give a series of lectures entitled "Languages of Paradise: Questions of Indo-European Historiography." Among those attending was Michel de Certeau (1925–1986), whose questions often led me to approach texts in fresh ways. My research continued at the Religious Sciences Division of the Ecole Pratique des Hautes Etudes, where Marcel Detienne and Charles Malamoud invited me to teach from 1986 to 1988. In the spring of 1989, I returned to the Ecole des Hautes Etudes, where I presented my most recent research in Yves Hersant's seminar. Over the years, these seminars have enabled me to clarify a number of points by attempting to answer questions raised by Georges Charachidzé, Maurice de Gandillac, Colette Guillaumin, Nicole Loraux, Jean-Pierre Peter, Jean Pouillon, and others.

Some of the ideas in this book were first presented in papers. In 1986 I took part in a conference, "Historiographical Investigation of Polytheisms," organized by Francis Schmidt, proceedings of which were published in *History and Anthropology* 3

(1987). Some points of my paper in that volume, "The Indo-European Mirror: Monotheism and Polytheism," pp. 327–374, are further developed here.

Yves Bonnefoy, who in April 1986 invited me to read a paper on "Vocations and Filiations" to his seminar at the Collège de France, focused my attention on more than one of the problems explored in this book.

I am indebted to Heinz Happ and Jacques Le Rider for stimulating conversations with German colleagues at the Seminar on Classical Philology at Tübingen and at a lecture delivered in June 1986 at the Franco-German Cultural Institute.

Finally, throughout these years, Willy Bok, director of the Martin Buber Institute at the Free University of Brussels, invited me to give lectures that were the occasion of much fruitful work.

Pierre Gothot kindly consented to be the first reader of my manuscript in preparation. Jacques Le Brun, Charles Malamoud, Nicole Loraux, Jean Bazin, Daniel Droixhe, and Pierre Vidal-Naquet commented on the completed manuscript. I wish to thank them, as well as Renate Schlesier, who reviewed all my translations from the German.

Published by the Ecole des Hautes Etudes en Sciences Sociales under the direction of Marc Augé, the manuscript was read by Jacques Revel, whom I thank for his friendly vigilance. At Editions du Seuil, Michel Chodkiewicz, recently succeeded by Claude Cherki, and Olivier Bétourné took charge of the book.

Finally, I wish to express my gratitude to Jean-Pierre Vernant, who took time from many pressing commitments to write a foreword.

M. O.

Chapter 1

Archives of Paradise

In the Garden of Eden, did Adam, Eve, God, and the serpent speak Hebrew, Flemish, French, or Swedish? Was Eden, through which a river with four branches flowed, situated in the east or the west, beside the Euphrates or on the banks of the Ganges? As theologians, philosophers, and philologists raced to discover what language was spoken in Paradise and to discern the contours of its miraculous geography, they strayed down many paths that have yet to be fully explored.

Although Augustine (354–430) favored the official view that Hebrew was the original "human language," dissident voices were already being heard in antiquity.[1] Theodoret of Cyrrhus (393–466?) placed his bet on Syriac, and Gregory of Nyssa (330?–394) was certain that Hebrew was not the most ancient tongue. Gregory insisted, in any case, that God was not, as some imagined him to be, a schoolmaster who taught the first humans their alphabet.[2]

During the Renaissance paradisaical languages cropped up in all corners of Europe. Controversy raged, as everywhere people proposed whatever idiom they ascribed to their own ancestors as the language of Eden.[3] In 1688 the Swede Andreas Kempe (1622–1689), who had been forced into exile by the Lutheran clergy of his native country, published in Hamburg a satirical pamphlet entitled *The Languages of Paradise*.[4] In a series of dialogues, he called attention to the comic aspects of the contest to populate Eden with many tongues. After discussing the learned works of his compatriots Georg Stiernhielm

(1598–1672) and Olaus Rudbeck (1630–1702), Kempe tells how "the voluptuous Eve" succumbed to the seductions of a satanic serpent speaking French.[5] This story of original sin continues in a garden that features, beside the francophone serpent, a Danish-speaking Adam and a Swedish-speaking God.

Early in the next century Georg Wilhelm Leibniz (1646–1716) wrote a treatise on the new science of comparative linguistics, of which he was one of the founders. He shared the view of a number of Renaissance and post-Renaissance writers who had revived the hypothesis that the languages of Europe had originated on a continent called Scythia.[6] This was the context in which the Indo-European idea originated, along with the hope of "shedding light on the origin of nations."[7] In this same text Leibniz writes of a "learned physician" from Antwerp, Jan van Gorp (1518–1572),[8] who was "not seriously mistaken in his view that the Germanic language, which he called Cimbric, bore as many marks of the primitive, if not more, than Hebrew itself."[9]

Playing with words, comparing phrases, proposing fantastic etymologies, van Gorp discovered in his native Flemish a number of survivals of the Adamic language and, along with many others, helped to develop the comparative method that has ever since been a staple of the human sciences.[10] Associated with the national awakening that led to various local rivalries between supposed primordial tongues, the idea that European languages shared a common ancestor gave rise, between the sixteenth and eighteenth centuries, to the concept of an abstract prototype, which in the nineteenth century took the ultimate form of the Indo-European hypothesis. Since then the idea of a primordial tongue has enjoyed a distinguished career: linguists have debated the nature of various primitive Indo-European dialects, while archaeologists have argued over the dwelling places of Indo-European tribes.[11]

Thus the search for the *Ursprache* and the hunt for the language of Paradise eventually diverged. One way to avoid confounding the two issues was to deny that Hebrew was the language of Eden. Richard Simon (1638–1712) was one scholar who carried on this dissident tradition, harking back to Gregory of Nyssa when he mocked "those who believe that God was the original author of the language that Adam and Eve spoke . . . as if God were a grammar teacher." [12]

Setting himself apart from other theologians, Simon also denies that "the Blessed will speak Hebrew in heaven." [13] After discussing various rivalries for the honor of being the "first language in the world," Simon notes that these controversies had political causes. [14] From the Church Fathers to his own contemporaries, "Nations fight for their languages." The Church, however, took a dim view of these debates. It favored the view of "the Jews, who are certain that Hebrew was the language of Adam." Despite doubts that are more than rhetorical, Simon finally comes down in favor of Hebrew, but with no real conviction: "In a word, the Hebraic language is simpler than Arabic and Chaldean, and both of these languages are simpler than Greek or Latin, so that if it is true that Adam spoke one of these languages, he probably spoke Hebrew" (p. 89).

In the late 1700s Johann Gottfried Herder (1744–1803) raised new questions and proposed answers that helped shape the Aryan-Semitic categories that would influence scholarship in the human sciences throughout the nineteenth century. Although Herder assigned Hebrew a special place as "one of the eldest daughters" of the *Ursprache*, [15] he also turned his attention to the heights of the "Indian mountains." [16] A glance at a "map of the world" enabled him to identify the Ganges as the "river of Paradise." [17]

While Herder followed the centuries-old tradition among biblical scholars linking philology and the geography of Paradise, [18] he nevertheless departed from tradition, like Simon, by insisting on the national aspect of these debates. After asking the traditional question, "Where was the garden?" (vol. 13, p. 431), Herder warned the reader against the dangers of such political-theological archaeology: "For every ancient nation likes to consider itself the firstborn and to take its territory for humanity's birthplace."

Taking his inspiration from Robert Lowth (1710–1788), Herder preferred to see in the structures of the Hebraic language the poetic source of Eden's miraculous topography. With Moses for his ally, Herder interpreted Genesis so as to subsume religion in a fiction of the sublime. The biblical story of Creation, he pointed out, says little about the geography of Paradise, which can therefore be seen as "the land of myth" (vol. 11, p. 323). Furthermore, Moses's imprecision is "proof of the truth" of this description (p. 324). Never having traveled in this miraculous region, Moses was too scrupulous to say more than the myth allowed. And even if he had visited the primordial place, Moses would have found there no "archives of Paradise." Herder therefore advised his contemporaries not to hold out for an archaeology of the impossible, not to play "saviors of the history" of Eden. Better "let the tradition subsist as a legend of the original world" and examine its consequences, for this is the story that lies "at the root of [Hebrew] poetry."

For Herder, then, the Hebrew Bible was poetry of an exemplary kind. Renan (1823–1892) preferred to see the Bible as the archives of humanity: "The primitive archives of this [Semitic] race, which by a remarkable twist of fate became the archives of the human race, have come down to us in Hebrew."[19]

Disputes over the origins of language and languages have not ceased to shape representations of human language.[20] Behind Herder's view lurks one of those conceptions according to which language is a kind of grid structuring thought and molding national character. Equally common are variations on the theme of language as a mirror, which reflects the images that form the soul of a people. Thus Herder looked upon language as a testimony to the development of the human mind, a repository of civilization's discoveries.[21] After all, Leibniz had included both individual and collective memory within the purview of linguistics when he affirmed that "languages are the best mirror of the human mind" and "the most ancient monuments of peoples."[22]

The inaccessible archives of Paradise evolved into the science of linguistics, which meditated upon language as a faithful witness to history that transcends the generations of humanity. In a 1759 dissertation entitled "On the Influence of Opinions on Language and of Language on Opinions" J. D. Michaelis (1717–1791) wrote: "Language is therefore a kind of archive in which human discoveries are protected against the most harmful accidents, archives that flames cannot destroy and that cannot perish unless an entire nation is ruined."[23]

By this time it had become impossible to speak of nations or national histories without discussing the instrument with which they maintained their identity over time and conveyed ancestral values from generation to generation: namely, language. A decade before Michaelis, Condillac (1715–1780) had done more than just initiate an academic debate when he identified language with "the genius of each people." Everything, he said, "confirms that each language expresses the character of the people that speaks it."[24]

Thus joined to the idea of the nation, language was considered the best source for discovering the distinctive traits of different peoples.[25] This method of writing national cultural history had been refined by several generations of scholars by the time Ferdinand de Saussure (1857–1913) looked back on the discipline of linguistics in the early twentieth century. He noted the "fairly widely accepted opinion that a language reflects the psychological character of a nation" before going on to state his objections to this received view.[26]

After Hebrew, Sanskrit

In the final years of the eighteenth century and in the first half of the nineteenth, the human sciences once again borrowed concepts from botany, biology, geology, and paleontology.[27] Sanskrit had supplanted Hebrew as the fashionable subject. In the salons and academies of France, England, and Germany, conversations about the language of the Vedas hastened the establishment of comparative linguistics by lending legitimacy to the newly formulated Indo-European hypothesis. For nineteenth-century historians the father of that hypothesis was William Jones (1746–1794). In a formal address delivered to the recently formed Asiatic Society of Calcutta on February 2, 1786, Jones, who had barely begun the study of Sanskrit,[28] announced the discovery of important linguistic affinities between Sanskrit, Greek, and Latin:

> The Sanscrit language, whatever be its antiquity, is of a wonderful structure; more perfect than the Greek, more copious than the Latin and more exquisitely refined than either; yet bearing to both of them a stronger affinity, both in the roots of verbs, and in the forms of grammar, than could possibly have been produced by accident; so strong, indeed, that no philologer could examine them all three, without believing them to have sprung from some common source, which, perhaps, no longer exists. There is a similar reason, though not quite so forcible, for supposing that both the Gothick and the Celtick, though blended with a very different idiom, had the same origin with the Sanscrit; and the old Persian might be added to the same family, if this were the place for discussing any question concerning the antiquities of Persia.[29]

Although some Europeans had long been aware of the existence of Sanskrit, and although certain parallels between Indian and Persian words and words from European languages (Italian, various German dialects, Greek, and Latin) had been explored since the sixteenth century, Jones's message was not received by the educated public until the beginning of the nineteenth century.[30] The first generation of Indo-Europeanists was influenced chiefly by a work of Friedrich von Schlegel (1772–1829), published in Heidelberg in 1808: *Essay on the Language and Wisdom of the Indians.*[31] In Paris the first chair in Sanskrit language and literature was established at the Collège de France for Antoine Léonard de Chézy (1773–1832) in 1814.[32] Two years later Franz Bopp (1791–1867) began work on his *Comparative Grammar* (1833–1849).[33] Freeing himself from the influences of his masters (who, like Schlegel, were also the precursors of romanticism), Bopp changed the course of Indo-European studies through his determination to create a system out of the guesswork of generations of scholars who had intuited the existence of a lost common ancestor for most European tongues.

The discovery of Indo-European caused a furor that extended well beyond the discipline of comparative philology. All the human sciences, from history to mythology, and soon to include "racial science," were affected by the discovery of a tongue that was known not only as Indo-European but also as Aryan. One of the leading promoters of Aryan theories, Friedrich Max Müller (1823–1900) described the inception of his discipline as the starting point for a new science of human origins: "Thanks to the discovery of the ancient language of India, Sanskrit as it is called . . . and thanks to the discovery of the close kinship between this language and the idioms of the principal races of Europe, which was established by the genius of Schlegel, Humboldt, Bopp, and many others, a complete revolution has taken place in the method of studying the world's primitive history."[34]

In other words, thanks to the new history of language, a study in which philology and linguistics made common cause, scholars now believed that they were in a position to make an accurate portrayal of prehistoric society. By comparative analysis of Indo-European linguistic roots, some scholars even hoped to uncover the words and deeds of mankind's earliest ancestors. Linguistic paleontology was the science of their dreams.

Yet Sanskrit, which lent credence to the idea of an Indo-European sphere of influence, did more than bestow scientific legitimacy on previous efforts of comparative research. The language of the Vedas fired the imagination of scholars driven by romantic curiosity about prehistoric times. Anticlericals, following the lead of Voltaire, who was fascinated by India, saw the shores of the Ganges as the source of mankind's most ancient philosophy.[35] But other scholars hoped to infuse new Aryan life into a Christianity that had suffered much at the hands of the Enlightenment and Revolution.

Some thinkers balked at the idea of replacing the biblical Eden with an Aryan Paradise. Among them was the young Ferdinand de Saussure, who turned his back on a community of European scholars entranced by visions of a prehistoric idyll. Reviewing the work of his teacher Adolphe Pictet (1799–1875) in 1878, Saussure wrote that "underneath research on the Aryas, that people of the golden age brought back to life by scholarly thought, was certainly an almost conscious dream of an ideal humanity."[36]

Salomon Reinach (1858–1932) also saw as the driving force behind much Indo-European research a yearning for the golden age that arose at "the boundary between imagination and science."[37] In his *Origins of the Aryans* (subtitled *History of a Controversy*), Reinach analyzed the works of scholars who, along with Pictet, produced "endless variations" on the theme of the Aryans' primitive state. "It seemed that a new Eden had been discovered beneath the fossil layers of language."[38]

The Orientalist James Darmesteter (1849–1894) reacted in a similar way to Indianists who looked upon the Vedas as the "primitive poetry of highly gifted shepherds." In a eulogy for Abel Bergaigne (1838–1888) Darmesteter pointed out that the eminent Sanskritist had departed from "scientific tradition," according to which the aim of philological research ought to be to discover the original philosophy of the Aryans: "European scholars, unwitting playthings of India's mythological illusions, customarily relegated the Vedas to the most ancient past, not just of history but of human thought. Brahmanic orthodoxy claimed contact through the Vedas with the earliest divine revelation. European scientific orthodoxy believed that through the Vedas it was in contact with the first appearance of religious thought in the Indo-European race. The Vedas became the sacred book of the religious origins of the race, the Aryan Bible."[39]

This history, which involved many of the key controversial issues of genealogical understanding in the West, had taken an unexpected turn in the late eighteenth century, when Hebrew, whose centrality had been challenged for some time, finally gave way to Sanskrit. Despite this demotion in the status of Hebrew, the West, still in search of ancestors, did not reduce its attachment to the language. Many nineteenth-century authors were able to convince themselves (if often only in part) to abandon faith in Genesis, but they did not give up on the possibility of a genealogy of human thought.[40] Familiarity with the Bible had made it possible to conceive of human existence as an uninterrupted expanse of time stretching from the Garden of Eden onward; now, as nineteenth-century philologists filled in the Indo-European archives, other texts with an air of eternity about them came to supplant the Bible. These Indo-European texts, like the Hebrew texts before them, were soon the subject of urgent questions and innumerable exegeses.

One contemporary witness to the romantic effusions of the early nineteenth century, G. W. F. Hegel (1770–1831), was critical of those who abandoned themselves to primitivism.

His comments attest to the shift from one notion of the "archives of Paradise" to another. The philosopher's views can be found in his *Philosophy of History* (1822–1831), where the fall of the first man symbolizes both the possibility of knowledge and the end of animal innocence. If the myth of original sin and Adam's fall is an account of man's earliest ancestors, then "Eden is a garden in which only animals can live thereafter, not men."[41]

In *Reason in History* (1830) Hegel considers the idea that civilization, perfect at its inception, has been in decline ever since. He criticizes the notion that we have access to the nature of primitive man through some kind of higher authority:

> This pretension takes up again the old notion of a primary, paradisaical state of man, which the theologians had elaborated after their fashion by asserting, for example, that God had spoken with Adam in Hebrew. This is today revised in accordance with other interests. [We are told that there existed a primitive people from whom we received our knowledge of science and art (Schelling; Schlegel, *The Language and Wisdom of the Indians*). This primordial people allegedly preceded the human race as such and was perpetuated in ancient legend in the guise of gods. Distorted vestiges of this people's high culture can allegedly be found in the most ancient myths. This theory, it is affirmed, is required by philosophy and supported by historical evidence.] The higher authority in question is the Biblical account. But this account, on the one hand, represents the primitive conditions only through the few traits that are known. . . . Yet these interpretations do not justify the opinion that a people has existed historically in such primitive conditions, and still less, that the pure knowledge of God and nature has been formed therein. Nature, so the fiction runs, originally stood open and transparent before the clear eye of man, as a bright mirror of divine creation, and the divine truth was equally open to him. . . . From this supposedly historical condition, then, all religions are said to have taken their origin.[42]

The "higher authority" alluded to by Hegel would continue to be invoked by the various schools of philology and comparative mythology through the end of the nineteenth century (Renan died in 1892, Max Müller in 1900). And it was invoked especially when scholars attempted to decipher the ways in which Providence had affected the course of history.

Technical Inventions

A lost language, an unknown people: from the remote Indo-European diaspora during a mythical-poetic age, nineteenth-century authors collected linguistic roots that stemmed, they assumed, from a time close to "the birth of language, almost at the creation of man."[43]

What to call this primitive continent destined to play a fundamental role in the development of the West?[44] What to name these new ancestors, over whom all Europe quarreled? Consensus on these issues was never achieved. Some authors changed terminology from one paragraph to the next: Aryans,[45] Indo-Germans,[46] Indo-Europeans.[47] Different scholars used the same terms interchangeably to refer to a people, a race, a nation, or a family of languages. Renan, for example, used both Aryan and Indo-European,[48] while Ignaz Goldziher (1850–1921) used Aryan and Indo-German (see Chapter 8). Other related terms included Japhetic,[49] "of Sanskrit stock," Indo-Classical, Arian,[50] Indo-Celtic, Thracian, and Caucasian, to name a few.[51]

This multifarious collection of names and concepts was contrasted with another fundamental grouping, the so-called Semitic languages. Long referred to as Aramaic or Oriental, these languages were named for Shem, the son of Noah and brother of Japheth (Gen. 5:32). Herder and A. L. von Schlözer (1735–1809) were the first to apply the term Semitic to a group of languages.[52]

The multitude of Indo-European tongues reflected the migratory abilities of the Indo-European peoples, who were great conquerors: their diaspora extended from India to the western extremities of Europe. The Semites, on the other hand, remained settled in one place and thus attached to their languages, cultures, and religions. Immobile in time as well as space, they played little if any part in what the nineteenth century saw as universal historical progress. The polytheistic dynamism of the Aryans was contrasted with the monotheistic stagnation of the Semites.

In the human sciences words can be conceptual tools. Whether borrowed from ancient traditions or forged for laboratory use, they reveal implicit presuppositions and goals. These functional terms may have been technical inventions, but at the same time they indicate the basic hypotheses of the new sciences.

Semitic did not apply only to Hebrew. Yet while the Arabic language and the Islamic religion could be seen as cardinal manifestations of Semitism, it was Hebrew—the language identified with the monotheistic religion it expressed—that inspired many of the questions that nineteenth-century scholars directed toward Semitic part of the globe.

Many specialists, for example, attributed to all Semitic groups characteristics ostensibly derived from the Hebrews of the historical period. As a corollary, Renan and many other nineteenth-century European scholars ascribed to the groups they called Aryan (or Indo-German or Indo-European) characteristics they attributed to the Greeks. Within the Aryan universe, the energy and abstract intellectual gifts of the Greeks prefigured the progress of the Indo-European world, while the Vedic pole represented the power of the primitive.

The negative content of anti-Semitism was directed essentially against those identified as descendants of the Hebrews—namely, the Jews—and not at all users of Semitic languages. Throughout Europe in the 1870s the terms Aryan and Semite embarked on new ideological and political careers outside philology and physical anthropology, but often referring to those disciplines for legitimacy. Vague and incendiary as these terms were, they continued in widespread use until 1945 and the collapse of Nazism.

In the preface to the second edition of *Comparative Grammar,* Bopp stressed the need for keeping the "idea of nationality" out of the new sciences of language: "I cannot approve the expression 'Indo-Germanic,' because I do not see why one should take the Germans as representatives for all the peoples of our continent when the point is to find a term broad enough to embrace so vast a family. . . . For now, in order to be more broadly understood, I shall use the term 'Indo-European,' which has already to some extent been consecrated by usage in France and England."[53]

These words were written in Berlin in August 1857. Today, except for universities in German-speaking countries, which have not heeded Bopp's advice, the term Indo-European is generally preferred, no doubt because, as Georges Dumézil (1898–1986) was fond of pointing out, it is so inadequate:

> All things considered, the inadequacy of the label in describing its object is precisely what recommends it: it is revealed as what it must be, a *conventional* sign . . . warning that it is the hypothesis of a community of origin, of a common heritage, that is the most plausible explanation for the correspondences that one can make out among such disparate historical facts. The goal of comparativists in linguistics as in other disciplines is thus a modest one, for they know that it is impossible to reconstruct the living drama of a common ancestral language or civilization because nothing can replace documents, and there are no documents.[54]

Forgetting History

Aryan and Semite: "two twins" at the origin of civilization.[55] Discovered in "the same cradle," they constitute a pair with unequal virtues. Separated in early childhood, Aryans and Semites follow singular destinies, are distinct in every way. In a divine drama whose theater is universal history, Providence sees to it that each plays its proper role. The Aryans bring the West mastery over nature, exploitation of time and space, the invention of mythology, science, and art, but the Semites hold the secret of monotheism—at least until that fateful day when Jesus comes into the world at Galilee.

This dual patrimony results in a dual heritage. The controversy between Jews and early Christians, in which the vocation of the disciples of the new Messiah clashed with the tradition of the Hebrews, found new formulations in the Aryan-Semitic discourse of the nineteenth century.

More explicitly in the work of some authors, less explicitly in that of others, the providential role of the historical pair shaped Indo-European and Semitic studies.[56] Renan, for example, envisioned a two-headed—Aryan and Semitic—civilization, and this view colored even his description of the landscape of Palestine, where a Semitic Judea stood out from, yet also mingled with, a Galilee that was less monotheistic, hence less Semitic and closer to Jesus (see Chapter 4).

Every discipline of the human and natural sciences was invited to contribute to the revelation of Providence's secrets. The growth of a positivist, critical spirit in historiography did not necessarily hamper the use of providential arguments to justify the course of events. Leopold von Ranke (1795–1886), who led the German historical school of his day, exemplifies this alliance of positivist methodology with religious explanation: "Every era," he said, "exists in an immediate relation to God."[57] In his own way Herder had already attempted to reconcile historical causality with the divine purpose that alone gives meaning to history. And in presenting Herder to French readers, Edgar Quinet (1803–1875) similarly proclaimed his faith in the providential sequence of events described by universal history.[58]

Science and religion in the nineteenth century thus shared more than one project.[59] Stripped of dogma and superstition, Christianity infused secular humanism with shared meaning. Although each scholar followed his own course, forming schools with others of like mind and opposing those with incompatible views, many confidently trod the paths of Providence. Allusion to Augustine was commonplace from Simon to Müller. Had not the Father of the Church, in the *City of God,* drawn a plausible picture of a remote past compatible with the novel categories of what was to become an influential theological system?[60]

A certain modernizing school within Christianity exchanged the "particular" for the "general" in order to restore the historical centrality of Christ.[61] The discourse of Aryan and Semitic must be understood within this historical context. The whole subject revived the old conflict between monotheisms, which Goldziher sought to quell. Once again the Christian tradition, even in secularized form, sought to distinguish itself from Judaism and Islam by reassigning roles and redrawing boundaries.[62]

In the nineteenth century science and Christianity attempted to find new ways to coexist, and interestingly enough the first "secular" science accepted by the Church was undoubtedly philology. Philology was a science born of endless debate. Heir to a rich legacy, to the treasures of the classical tradition and biblical exegesis, it soon revealed its importance: matters of dogma turned on philological issues, on grammatical details.[63] Although it is true that "the birth of philology attracted far less notice in the Western mind than did the birth of biology or political economy," the discipline nevertheless left an indelible mark on Western visions of history.[64] Yet it was a science that was by no means open to history.

Limited at first to the Indo-European languages, comparative philology frequently neglected history. Taking inspiration from the botanical model, the linguist ambled about the gar-

den of languages gathering linguistic roots.[65] Soon these roots
metamorphosed into rigid structures that could not be eroded
by time. Saussure's *Course in General Linguistics* begins with a
brief look at the history of the subject, in which he notes that
comparative grammar "was exclusively comparative instead of
historical."[66] Conscious of the "irresistible logic of the linguistic fact," Saussure calls for the development of a comparative
method that would not resign itself to doing without history.[67]
While it is true, he concedes, that historical reconstruction in
grammar is based on comparison, comparison by itself does not
justify any conclusion "Conclusive results eluded these com-
parativists all the more because they viewed the development
of two languages as a naturalist might view the growth of two
plants. . . . This exclusively comparative method led to a
whole series of erroneous conceptions. . . . Language was
viewed as a unique sphere, a fourth kingdom of nature. . . .
Today no one can read eight or ten lines written in those days
without being struck by the peculiarity of the ideas and the
terms used to justify them."[68] Naturalistic models not only
removed the effects of history from language but also made it
possible to stereotype civilizations, which came to be identified
with ideas about their linguistic systems.

Among the Semites the Hebrews were credited with a
"higher form" of rationality, and this was adduced as grounds
for excluding them from profane history: arbiter and bearer of
a truth that time could not diminish, required eternally to bear
witness, the Hebrew people were exempted from change.

Goldziher, the pioneer of Islamic studies, was the first to
undertake comparative work on the Semitic languages, in
which he hoped to place the Old Testament on the same foot-
ing as other texts. He invited European scholars to rescue the
Hebrews from the paradise to which they had been relegated,
outside history's gates. He insisted that Bible stories be allowed into the preserve of comparative mythology along with

the legends of other peoples and thus included in the stream of history.

In a different sphere we find another reason for the ambivalence that always plagued Indo-European studies, torn between structure and history. To the authors who used it, the notion of a "family of languages" meant demonstrating the existence of affinities among different language groups. These linguistic affinities were then justified either by historical and geographical connections between peoples (with a consequent implication of systematic borrowings) or by the idea of descent from a common ancestor to account for the existence of common word roots and grammatical structures. Some authors combined both arguments, and to this day the ambiguity persists in the form of a tension between typological models and historical arguments.[69]

My hope in the following pages is to restore some of the complexity of the work of Herder, Renan, and Goldziher. The best way to understand them is no doubt to take them seriously, even to "succumb to their spell,"[70] rather than attempt to impose a logic alien to their time. "One must resist the temptation, to which too many historians of science succumb, to make the often obscure, clumsy, and even confused ideas of the ancients more accessible by translating them into a modern language that makes them clearer at the cost of distortion."[71] Occasionally one can arrest a thought in its flight by identifying the questions that gave rise to a particular text, or by tracing changes in the problems scholars set themselves, or by attending to unexpected metaphors and associations of images.

Attempts to bring the components of the Aryan-Semite pair together—despite the occasional emphasis placed on convergences, and despite the rather surprising light in which the pastor R. F. Grau (1835–1893) cast the nineteenth-century history of the pair—never overcame the contrasting ways in which each was approached. By the same token, emphasizing one or another aspect of Renan's work cannot conceal the fact that it is structured around a dynamic of contradictions. A scholar's writings can be a place where conflicts crystallize: an author's whole work can be based on positions that to us seem mutually contradictory. Herder and Renan could take a historical approach at one point only to abandon it at another; they could defend nationalist or racist views in one place, only to criticize such views elsewhere.

To confine an author to a simple image of his work, often concocted by later researchers for purposes of their own, is to recreate the past by inventing precursors for the present.[72] Renan, who has traditionally been cast as the champion of an exclusively secular science of religion, is a case in point; he will not be confined to that role here.

To take an author seriously, to view his work in the context of its times, to attempt to describe the twists and turns of his thinking does not, however, mean that one agrees with his conclusions or subscribes to his views. Obvious as this point is, it is worth making explicitly here.

The sources on which this book is based invite us to consider Aryans and Semites as a functional pair with a providential aspect, as elements of a theory of the origins of civilization (in the sense in which that word was used by the authors in question). Except in rare instances I make no effort to point out the odious uses to which some of the texts I study were put, in some cases soon after they were written (during the Dreyfus affair, for example).

The plain truth of the matter is that, in the heart of Europe in the middle of the twentieth century, the words Aryan and Semite became labels of life and death for millions of men, women, and children classed as one or the other. Historians of anti-Semitism, of whom Léon Poliakov was one of the pioneers in France, have tried to understand these old arguments and

ration from methods perfected by natural scientists, and
adopted the new perspective of comparative studies, they continued to be influenced by the biblical presuppositions that
defined the ultimate meaning of their work. Despite differences in outlook, Renan, Max Müller, Pictet, and many others
joined romanticism with positivism in an effort to preserve a
common allegiance to the doctrines of Providence.

Against this backdrop of teleological history, the discovery
of an evident kinship between the European languages and
Sanskrit suddenly brought the Far East closer to the West. The
Semitic Near East was now juxtaposed with a new Indo-
European Orient. In order to describe the earliest stage of human intelligence, philologists and mythologists invented Aryans and Semites, to whom they invariably ascribed opposing,
if sometimes complementary, roles. Many scholars found it
easy to think of themselves as the descendants of this providential couple at the root of the only civilization they considered
worthy of the name: Semites by spiritual filiation, Aryans by
historical vocation.

Before contemplating their own image in the Aryan mirror,
however, the scholars of Western Christendom had thoroughly
explored the relations between the Old and the New Testament, between Hebrew, Greek, and Latin. At stake was control of a legacy that hinged on a few vowels of dubious significance, said to contain a providential history, preliminary to a
radiant future.

their more recent uses.[73] Proliferating investigations o
in all its forms have begun to shed light on the role tha
philosophical and historical traditions may have playe
development of ideologies and policies that gave rise–
some cases still do give rise—to violence.[74]

The goal of this book is more modest: to investi|
work of selected scholars in order to bring out the force
lying discussion of the terms Aryan and Semite up t
the year of Renan's death and two years before the :
Captain Dreyfus.[75] In order to penetrate to the coheren
of these various theories, I shall examine how each autl
to formulate problems which he then attempted to sol·

The authors selected as the focus of individual chapt
chosen because (with the exception of Grau) they seem
to be pathbreakers, men whose work was innovative ai
ential. Their writings do not constitute a closed corpi
ever, and this book is to be read as a report on res
progress.[76] Its title, *The Languages of Paradise,* is emble:
is meant to call attention to the importance of scholarl
concerning the primal languages, whose study was c
the inception of the science of linguistics and, particu
Indo-European studies.

Long confined to the realm of theology, controver:
origins—of language, religion, society, and civili:
spilled over into secular discourse and kindled count
putes as the human sciences began to flourish in the ni
century. Hegel, as we have seen, described the mome
the theology of origins was transformed into a histor
primal, in response to "other interests" and new expec

The authors of the nineteenth century were hostage
are no doubt too, to the questions they set themselves.
they cast aside the old theological questions, they r
attached to the notion of a providential history. Althou
borrowed the techniques of positivist scholarship, too

🐾 Chapter 2

Divine Vowels

On May 16, 1707, *Le Journal des Sçavans* announced to its readers "a very important discovery" made in K'ai-feng in the province of Hunan, China: "a synagogue founded before the birth of Jesus Christ; Jews to whom the Savior was unknown" (p. 256). People began to imagine an archaic synagogue, "prior to the destruction of Jerusalem or even to the Incarnation."[1] They believed that an authentic version of the fundamental text of Christian monotheism was about to be unearthed, the original of the Hebrew Bible in all the purity and splendor of its Mosaic writing. This belief was based on the opinion of "some learned men" that the Jews of the Talmudic era, "enemies of the Christians, altered the Holy Books . . . to bring their meaning into conformity with the prejudices of their sect."[2] Unlike the corrupt Bible the Jews had spread among the nations of Europe, the integrity of the K'ai-feng Text seemed to be assured. It was protected by China's unbroken history: from the time "the Lord dictated the law to [Moses] so quickly that he had no time to put in the marks" (that is, the Hebrew vowels), to the time the Jesuits came upon the Jews of K'ai-feng, no messianic event had intervened in China to disrupt the course of time.[3] The inviolate and homogeneous expanse of Chinese history was expected to contain the secrets of Providence.

This initial enthusiasm was ultimately equalled by the final disappointment. The hope that these Chinese Jews would turn out to be guardians of the golden age, uncontaminated by their brothers of the diaspora, collapsed on October 25, 1723, when Jean Domenge, a Jesuit and Hebrew scholar, stated in his letter that "the Text of their Bible is identical to the Text of the Amsterdam Bible."

The quest for the correct version, the search for the original, was a chronic concern of the churchmen who administered the memory of Christendom, as it would later become a chronic concern for nineteenth-century philologists. Everything hinged on this search for the providential text dictated verbatim by God to Moses, or at any rate for the "lesson" closest to the original. Since the Reformation, which reaffirmed the principle of "verbal inspiration" to support the assertion that the Bible is unique and infallible, the debate had grown.[4] The obsession that emerged in that spring 1707 issue of *Le Journal des Sçavans*—to restore the original purity of the inaugural text— had long roots, going back at least to the Church Fathers.

Some thirty years had passed since one of the founders of modern exegesis, the Oratorian Richard Simon (1638–1712), had revived old questions about the integrity of the biblical text. In his *Critical History of the Old Testament* (1678), Simon examined the motives that might have caused men of the Church to portray the Jews as counterfeiters of Holy Scripture. Some authors maintained that "the Jews maliciously corrupted their copies" of the Bible to justify their denial of the Christian Messiah's irruption into history.[5] Falsifying prophesies, they "abridged their chronology" and manipulated historical time in order to prove that the Messiah had not yet come. Simon also cited a second reason for doubting the authenticity of the Hebrew text: "The Church at its inception received no version of Holy Scripture other than the Greek Septuagint" (p. 102).

In these circumstances it was only natural for the first Christians, confronted with an alternate version of the sacred text, to accuse the Jews of having altered Holy Writ. In summary Simon argued that "this prejudice of the Fathers came solely from the fact that they recognized no authentic Bible other than the Greek version of the Septuagint." For them there was no question that anything not found in their text was a distortion. Whatever was not written down in the Septuagint, the only "authentic and divine" Scripture, was the result of corruption (p. 104).

Accusations of corruption thus flew back and forth between Jews and Christians and between rival Christian communities. Over the centuries various versions and canonical translations of the sacred text saw their fortunes rise and fall. In 1546 the Council of Trent recognized the Vulgate as the sole authentic text. More than a century later, Simon, encouraged by the Counter-Reformation (whose work the Oratorian Fathers had been formed to carry on), proposed a new reading in his *Critical History,* but it failed to take hold. Bossuet (1627–1704) had only to glance at the table of contents on Holy Thursday (April 7, 1678) to come to the conclusion that the work deserved to be consigned to flames. What piece of impudence had caused him to declare the book "a compilation of impieties and a bulwark of libertinage?"[6] The heading to the fifth chapter of Book 1 was enough: "Proof of additions and other changes that have been made to the Bible, and in particular to the Pentateuch. Moses cannot be the author of everything in the books attributed to him. Various examples."

No sooner was the book printed than all extant copies were seized, banned by the King's Council, and consigned to the flames. On May 21, 1678, Father Simon was notified of the decree expelling him from the Oratory.

The Secrets of Pronunciation

One year before Simon's treatise appeared, Baruch Spinoza (1632–1677) died, some twenty years after his expulsion from the synagogue of Amsterdam on July 27, 1656. Although Spinoza and Simon had very different outlooks and disagreed in profound ways, both contributed to the upheaval in biblical criticism.[7]

Spinoza's *Posthumous Works* (1677), published a few months after his death, contain a *Short Treatise on Hebrew Grammar*, an uncompleted work that is never included in French editions of Spinoza's complete works. At the beginning of this text Spinoza writes: "In Hebrew the vowels are not letters. That is why the Hebrews say that 'vowels are the soul of letters' and that letters without vowels are 'bodies without soul' [both images taken from the *Zohar*]. In truth, the difference between letters and vowels can be explained more clearly by taking the example of the flute, which is played with the fingers. The vowels are the sound of the music; the letters are the holes touched by the fingers."[8]

Comprehension of the Hebrew Bible depends on the vowels. Represented by diacritical marks below or above the letters of the text, the vowels set the text in motion and bestow sound and meaning. Simon, who analyzes the theological and historical consequences of the vowel issue, points out that the early Christians often lacked knowledge of Hebrew and that this ignorance may have been one reason why prejudice against the Jewish conservators of the text was able to take root (p. 103).

The Hebrew word is described as mute, an opaque substance whose occult meaning emerges only when it is voiced. In order to be read, the text must be chanted, infused with animating breath according to rules distilled from centuries of vocalization. The meaning of a verse becomes clear only when, with the help of this prolonged oral tradition, the light of the vowels is made to shine upon the dark body of the text. According to Simon, it was not until quite late (around the seventh century C.E., in fact), that the Jewish scholars known as Masoretes wrote down the vowel marks that fixed the vocalization of the text through a system of signs (pp. 131–135).[9] Now, this "Masora was in no sense divine" (p. 353), and "the Masoretes might have been mistaken in infinitely many places." While they were no doubt learned men, they were not, Simon notes, "either prophets or infallible" (p. 354).

The divine text, the sign of Providence, was thus modulated by vowels of human inspiration. The question of this "melody" of diacritics, borne of generations of custom and tradition, is fundamental.[10] The whole textual edifice of the Hebrew Bible in fact rests on how consonants are vocalized. Simon points out that in Hebrew, as in Arabic or Syriac, to change the punctuation of a text is to change its meaning (p. 287). Since reading the Bible depends on these vowel marks, it is impossible to believe "that the Holy Scripture is entirely the word of God, since it is partly the invention of men" (p. 146). This was a scandalous state of affairs, and Simon, eager to lessen the shock of his argument, was eventually forced to invoke Providence.

Simon first points out that the meaning that men imparted to the text when they originally noted down the vowels depended on an ancient tradition. The deciphering of Scripture was therefore "authorized by custom" (p. 148). Nevertheless, the rules of interpretation were not sufficient to prevent "grammarian rabbis from arguing even today about the roots of numerous words" (p. 171). Like all readers, the rabbis did not avoid all the pitfalls of the language, such as words containing "hidden or added letters" (p. 170). The still latent meaning of the text therefore depends on the punctuation: therein lies "the greatest secret of the Hebraic language."

Thus Simon's critique turned on uncertainties in the interpretation of the biblical text. It was precisely because there was no Hebrew version "constant through the centuries" (p. 355) that one could and even should subject the Bible to vigorous criticism. Scholars, Simon tells us at the very beginning of his book, should "apply themselves to criticism of the Bible and correct the mistakes in their copies" (p. 1). He then invokes the authority of Augustine, who also advocated "this sort of criticism."

In order to improve and "repair the Hebrew text" (p. 356), elementary rules of comparison are to be applied to the available versions. For while "no one can deny that the Hebrew text is the original" (p. 353), it must be conceded that the extant copies are "defective." Whenever possible, therefore, he recommends that "the Hebrew text be corrected . . . the original perfected." The critical technique for accomplishing this feat is made all the more necessary by a loss as irremediable as it is providential: "The first originals have been lost" (p. 1). Simon's prescription is radical: to work tirelessly to restore the inspired Scripture to its initial form in order to "reestablish, insofar as possible, this first original" (p. 353).

Simon is here indulging in the kind of philological speculation that Christian theological controversy had often fostered over the centuries. The belief that the Bible was divinely inspired, that its text was drafted under the influence or with the aid of the Holy Spirit, was compatible with at least two hypotheses. On the one hand the Bible might be the result of an immediate revelation: Holy Scripture was literally dictated to Moses, and then to the Prophets, by God. These scribes were in a sense mere "secretaries of the Holy Spirit." [11] According to this "verbal inspiration," each word was noted down under divine dictation. On the other hand, the Bible might have been drafted under divine guidance: the authors, though still "guided by the Spirit of God," might then have made use of their own verbal expressions. [12] By taking this second view, Simon was able to separate the actual inspiration of the biblical books from the question of the authenticity of particular passages open to "further perfecting." The Bible had to be divinely inspired, but that did not prevent Simon from admitting that there might have been, here and there, compilations, additions, or even errors of composition. [13]

By stressing this instability of the Bible Simon sought to dispel the mystery of how a revealed text could be at once authentic and distorted. Everyone, he says, whether Jew or Christian, recognizes that the Bible is the "pure Word of God" (p. 1). Nevertheless, since time immemorial, men have been the custodians of the sacred books "as well as books of all other kinds." Since the first originals are missing, and since all books are subject to the ravages of time and space, there must have been changes due to the "length of time" and the "negligence of the copyists."

Simon considers these transformations of the text as effects of divine Providence, the force that animates history and imposes mutability on Scripture. He presses this crucial observation further by arguing that examples of the "authentic" Bible, that is, copies in conformity with scriptural doctrine, "cannot be suspected of corruption even though they may in fact have been corrupted" (p. 495). The critic brushes aside the paradox in this formulation and attempts to resolve the problem in the spirit of Paul: "The Providence of God preserved Scripture in the Church by preserving the purity of the doctrine, not by preventing corruption in copies of the Bible" (p. 495). Since "faith can subsist without Scripture," the Church provides the securest shelter for the doctrine that establishes the "limits" (p. 494) of the authenticity of the text.

Thus God had chosen not to preserve "the first originals of the Bible in their entirety" (p. 495). In a chapter devoted to a critique of "England's polyglot Bible," Simon says that he is simply following in the footsteps of the Church Fathers when he distinguishes between the documentary value of the text and the truth of Scripture, an original truth entrusted to the Church by God: "When Saint Paul said that the Church was the pillar and prop of truth, his words went unheeded by the grammarians and critics who have revised copies of the Bible. But he was attempting to point out that the truth of religion must not be sought anywhere but in the Church, which alone possesses Scripture because it possesses the true meaning. Hence even if there were no copies of the Bible in the world, religion would not cease to be preserved, because the Church would still exist. Such was the Fathers' view of the matter" (p. 489).[14]

In other words, as long as the "melody" was sung by a chorus of voices in unison, the Bible could be read and its providential message understood. In this way the polyvalent quality of the Hebrew vowels did not affect the interpretation of the text, which was therefore saved from confusion. The unique meaning of Holy Scripture would emerge from the harmony imposed by doctrine, which was transmitted by the Church rather than by an irrevocably absent text. Though the Bible might exist in many versions, the critic must always remember that God entrusted "to his Church the true doctrine to which the books of Scripture must conform" (p. 495).

When faced with the uncertainties that, like the vowel marks indicating melodic modulations, adorned the biblical text, exegetes frequently replied with a single-minded philological incantation: their purpose was to restore to the sacred books of the Bible, damaged by human negligence and historical vicissitude, the divine meaning that informed their writing. Always their goal was to perfect the capacity to decipher the signs of Providence.

The Poetry of the Sublime

Following Spinoza and Richard Simon, and despite opposition from Catholics and Protestants, other authors embarked on a variety of unofficial exegeses, although it is not always possible to trace influences and crosscurrents between generations.[15] New readings tampered with chronology to one degree or another and emphasized different values in the ancient text, and before long new uses of the documents were authorized, although their divine character was jealously maintained. Whereas Simon had examined the most minute transformations of the Hebrew text in order to reveal different stages of composition and call attention to alterations, later authors embarked on a literary analysis of divine Scripture.

Employing the same aesthetic criteria that had been applied to Greek and Latin classics since the Renaissance, Robert Lowth (1710–1788) treated the Old Testament as a sublimely inspired poem. Compared with the classics, the simple, naive images of the Hebrew Bible were striking. The poetry of the Bible was a secret poetry, whose divine meaning had to be deciphered; this was the task Lowth set himself in his *Lectures on the Sacred Poetry of the Hebrews.* [16] His aim was to single out poetic images that would offer the reader immediate access to the biblical text. Simple in style, this sacred poetry bore the mark of the sublime (p. 277), whose categories Lowth applied to what he saw as the essence of religious expression. [17]

What of "profane poets" (p. 299)? They are also "sublime geniuses," yet they remain "purely human." In no way can they be considered the equals of, or even be compared to, the sacred poets (p. 256). The divine poetry of the Bible was the work of "sacred writers" (p. 298) with a dual nature, profane as well as sacred. Though inspired by the Holy Spirit, they nevertheless retained their own character, their own peculiar genius: "In fact their souls are not so dominated by divine influence that what man takes from nature is totally destroyed . . . and although the writings of Moses, of David and Isaiah, everywhere exude something so elevated, so divine, that they appear clearly to have been dictated by the spirit of God, we nevertheless still recognize Isaiah, David, and Moses" (p. 298). [18]

Although Lowth begins his *Lectures* by pointing out that poetry, unlike philosophy, "instructs with the aid of pleasure" (p. 11), he also knows that certain difficulties must be overcome before the "grace" (p. 101) of the Old Testament can be recognized. These difficulties are inherent in a text bristling with novel expressions that allude to ways of living, thinking, and feeling associated with the "most ancient people that ever existed" (p. 97). In order to penetrate to the "innermost feelings" of this Hebrew people, who inhabited a planet astronomically distant from eighteenth-century Christians,[19] Lowth exhorted his readers to transcend the centuries by identifying with the authors and even with the original audience of these marvelous tales. To appreciate the singular elegance of the text, at once so familiar through religion yet so distant in space and time, we must approach it through the eyes of the ancient Hebrews: "We must, as it were, see everything with their eyes, judge everything in terms of their opinions, and above all make every effort, in reading the works of the Hebrews, to become Hebrews ourselves" (pp. 97–98).[20] Only then can we glimpse the sacred unity of this ancestral poetry.

While Lowth regarded study of "the genius of the language of the Hebrews" (p. 97) as tantamount to an interplanetary voyage, he did not find it necessary to depart from the paths of scholarship sanctioned by Protestant authorities. As bishop of Oxford and later London, he, along with other scholars in England, France, and Germany, exemplified a new form of orthodoxy, which combined Christian exaltation of the Old Testament with scholarly exploration of the Hebrew tongue. Lowth himself pointed out how munificent God had been since the Reformation in bestowing blessings on scholars who unearthed the treasures hidden in the Bible.[21] By liberating Hebrew from the synagogue these religious experts had transcended space and time to restore to the language of the Old Testament its original power. The exegete, who in Lowth's imagination explored the text like an astronomer seeking to discover unknown stars, was no longer obliged to settle for substitutes for the original or to follow "blindly those blind guides, the Jewish doctors."[22] The vowels, now emancipated from rabbinical tradition, could at last sing the Church of Christ. Far from being infallible, the Masora ceased to be regarded as an edifice built "on the rock of divine authority." On the contrary, the old science of vowels turned out to have been forged "by clumsy hands and built on sand." To guard against hermeneutic distortion of the providential text, Lowth hoped to offer his reader a poetics whose clerical intensity was guaranteed by a philology of the sublime.

The Most Singular *Elohim*

Herder addressed his treatise *On the Spirit of Hebrew Poetry* (1782–1783) "to lovers of the most ancient, simplest, most sublime poetry that ever was" (vol. 11, p. 215).[23] Because the work of the celebrated Bishop Lowth was known, Herder tells us, to "everyone," he would not imitate it but would try instead to make an original contribution to "knowledge of the progress of things divine and human."

Born on the shores of the Gulf of Riga off the Baltic Sea, Johann Gottfried Herder (1744–1803) was one of the forerunners of German Romanticism. A disciple of Immanuel Kant (1724–1804) and Johann Georg Hamann (1730–1788), he wrote voluminously on many subjects, including science, art, theology, and political and social thought.[24] He was a man fascinated by the origins and uniqueness of individual cultures, and at one time or another idealized the Hebrews, the Egyptians, and the Brahmans of India.[25]

Herder wrote around the same time that William Jones and his friends were delighting in the discovery of Sanskrit literature and founding the Asiatic Society of Calcutta.[26] It is against this historical background that Herder's enthusiastic works are best understood.

Although his passion for the primordial, the *Ur,* predominated in his late eulogy to the splendor of the Hebrew tongue, Herder did not consider Hebrew to be the "language of Paradise." [27] He thought of it not as "the mother of all languages" but as "one of the eldest daughters" of the *Ursprache,* or primal language. An "echo of the most ancient times" could consequently still be heard in Hebrew poetry.

Herder's fascination with things archaic was already apparent in his reflections *On the Origin of Language* (1770), where he plays on the words *morgenländisch* (oriental) and *ursprünglich* (original). [28] Here Hebrew shines forth as an "Orient of mankind," as the Lutheran pastor alludes to "the breath of God," his metaphor for the sounding of the vowels omitted from the Hebrew text. For if the vowel is "what is primary and most vital, the linchpin of all language," in Hebrew it is embodied by nothing more than "airy breath," invisible to the eye but "captivating to the ear." So spiritual and ethereal is this breath that it cannot be encoded by any alphabet. A light emanating from the flickering, indefinite text illuminates the face of its reader. Its invisible structure manifests the unimaginable, untouchable face of God.

The same devotion is to be found in Herder's *Spirit of Hebrew Poetry* (1782), which begins with a dialogue between Alciphron, who is dubious of the virtues and benefits of Hebrew poetry, and Eutyphron, who not only demonstrates the prodigious universality of the language but also shows how Hebrew grammar conveys divine messages. [29] Alciphron expresses his astonishment that anyone can take a serious interest in so impoverished a language. Isn't this vowelless tongue "like a dead hieroglyphics that often lacks a key" to its meaning or even its pronunciation (vol. 11, p. 226)?

Alciphron repeatedly asks what has happened to the vowels. Eutyphron finally elaborates his view. He concedes that the known Hebrew vowels were probably added by the rabbis at a relatively late date. But surely Hebrew must have had vowels from the beginning; it is inconceivable to think otherwise. "Who could write letters without the breath that gives them a soul, when everything depends on that inspiration?" (p. 240). In oriental languages, where "breath" symbolizes the movements of the soul, images and sensuous expressions are contained in "word roots" (p. 230). Primal languages are similar: the older they are, the closer the word roots are to the senses. Hebrew is in this respect exemplary: "poor in abstractions but rich in sensory representations" (p. 228). Its poverty is an attribute of its archaic splendor, just as the simplicity of its poetic style is a mark of the sublime.[30]

In his *Treatise on the Origin of Language* Herder characterizes primal languages in terms of five propositions (vol. 5, pp. 70ff). Human nature, he says, is "a tissue of language" (p. 68).[31] He then argues that if human reason requires abstraction, and if abstraction requires articulate language, then language must be the vehicle of reason among all peoples. He insists that "every grammar is nothing but a philosophy of language" (p. 82). Now we can understand why Herder was so interested in primitive linguistic systems: the less grammar a language has, the richer it is in images. The less abstract, the greater its poetic resources. Crude as "the first lexicon of the human soul" may have been, it was shaped by perception of nature's sounds and hence capable of producing a luxuriant poetry. In such circumstances it is easy to see how the roots of words grew out of the "dictionary of nature" (p. 83).

Similar statements can be found in the dialogues that Herder included in his *Spirit of Hebrew Poetry.* After listening to an exposition of the structure *(Bau)* of the Hebrew language (vol. 11, p. 227), Alciphron turns the conversation to an even more controversial subject. He asks what meaning is to be attributed to traces of polytheism found in the Hebrew tongue, a polytheism that lurks at the heart of Hebrew poetry, in the very first words of Genesis. Was it not to avoid the polytheism "charac-

teristic of all uncultivated nations" (p. 253) that Moses used
the plural *Elohim* (Lords) with a singular verb in the phrase
"Elohim created?"

Eutyphron reassures his interlocutor: while the *Elohim* may
have been spirits that accompanied the Creation, they never
tempted the Hebrews with polytheism. The idea of a single
God always protected Hebrew poetry and bestowed upon it
nobility, truth, and a wisdom that, "happily, has become mis-
tress of the world" (p. 255). The oneness of God "is the most
ancient barrier against idolatry," against the vices and terrors
that "promote disorder among the gods."

Herder then expresses amazement that despite so much
identity and oneness, this divine poetry is never monotonous.
On the contrary, it is full of images and personifications and
alive with natural phenomena, with the force of the winds and
the flash of lightning. In a comparative history of poetry, no
one could possibly confuse this Hebrew poetry born of monotheism with the "monstrous chaos" (p. 265) of the Greeks, a
chaos that predated the formation of the world, when "the atoms danced to and fro." In the poetry of the Hebrews a single
ray of light was enough to bring order to chaos, separating
heaven from earth and assigning each creature to its proper
sphere.

Guide and protector of civilization, the "first precocious impulse" (vol. 12, p. 32) of the poetics that gave it voice, monotheism was for Herder the surest barrier against polytheistic
disorder. This unique principle left its imprint on Hebrew, in
which we recognize "the eye of providence." The language, a
"masterpiece of perceptible concision and order" (pp. 27–28),
inaugurated "the original logic." A savage people could not
have spoken it, let alone have written Genesis.

Herder does not shirk the delicate question of the represent-
ability of God, the "invisible instructor" of the human race.
How can it be that, despite Moses's total ban on the worship of

images, God appeared? And in what form, since the man on Mount Sinai never saw Jehovah, but only a "flame in a burning bush?" (p. 34). Herder answers that Jehovah, though invisible, manifested himself through his name, each of his various denominations having its own distinct value. The visible sign whereby God manifested himself became "the messenger of his gaze" (p. 35). The apparitions of the divine are therefore above all products of a legible text animated by the breath of the vowels—that invisible component which charms the ear. This was possible simply because the Hebrew language made it possible to perceive the invisible both as pure appearance and as the paradigm of all poetry.

Animated by a minimum of grammar, a limpid vocabulary, and an abundance of images and sensations, Hebrew poetry was rooted in a genius at once "human and divine" (p. 6). Just as the superhuman inspiration of the Bible found expression in individual narratives whose authors are identifiable by their style, Hebrew poetry owed everything to its dual nature.[32] Indeed, if "God created the source of emotion in man" by giving humans the faculty to express themselves in poetic language, "the origin of poetry" can be called divine. But just as sensations experienced by the prophets as a result of divine influences necessarily took the form of human sentiments, it has to be admitted that poetry is also "of exclusively human origin" (p. 7). Thus Genesis, the first piece of poetry to be preserved, is "a vast canvas of images," a glimpse of the inchoate universe organized according to principles of human perception.

The Hebrew language, "replete with the respiration of the soul" (vol. 11, p. 232), also possessed other qualities that suited it for poetry. Like children "who want everything at once" (p. 234), the Hebrews "expressed person, number, time, action, and more with a single sound." Their verbs had only two tenses, aorists floating between past and future, resulting in the indefinite suspension of time from which Hebrew poetry

stemmed. For Herder, this single mood, this absence of multiple orientations in time, this "action which distinguishes no
time" (p. 233) constituted a crucial feature of the language. It
was what enabled the Hebrews to make pure poetry of history,
for the language was spared the "historical style" (p. 234) that
develops when verbs can be conjugated according to time and
mood.

This state of language naturally corresponded to a certain
type of society. The "legends of Paradise" (vol. 12, p. 29) were
"pastoral tales" *(Hirtensagen)*. Müller and Pictet would also
have occasion to speak of shepherds, and they, too, would find
words of praise for a language of immediacy, transparent and
grounded in images.[33] For them, however, the scene of Paradise was peopled with actors speaking not Hebrew but Aryan.
They did not simply borrow Herder's model and change the
cast. Unlike Herder's "poor pastors" of the Orient (vol. 11,
p. 229), who revel in their splendid poetic powers but have no
future, the ancestors of Aryan civilization were portrayed as
heralds of progress, looking forward to a bright future for the
Christian West and the modern world.

Hebrew—that wonderfully poetic tongue of adult children,
that primal speech—exists, in Herder's view, only within the
confines of an archaic geography, where, before ending in the
"sad mélange" of the diaspora, Hebrew was "the living language of Canaan." Eutyphron insists that in that distant past,
at least, this pastoral tongue was like "an impoverished yet
beautiful and pure country girl" (p. 230). We must forgive it
if, in its wretched dispersion, it borrowed "the finery of its
neighbors." In other words, the enchanted tongue of the Hebrews has nothing to do with the language spoken by their
descendants of the Talmudic era.

Chapter 3

The Cycle of the Chosen Peoples

To reinforce his argument in the second part of *The Spirit of Hebrew Poetry* (vol. 12), Herder abandoned the dialogue form and expanded his view beyond the virtues of the archaic. Hebrew poetry, like the temple according to Jewish law, was, he said, utterly devoid of images of the divine and shorn of all idols: "For God is present and active among his people solely through laws" (p. 88).

Herder's *poetics,* his aesthetic of the Hebrew language and style, thus led him to a discussion of the *politics* of this ancient oriental text.[1] Who were all these "sacred poets" (p. 40) if not prophets? And was not the first of them named Moses, the *Nomokrator* or Lawgiver (p. 299)? It was to Moses that God "made a sign" (p. 34), revealing himself in a form that became "the soul of the poetry" of the prophets. Herder's five hundred and more pages devoted to praise of Hebrew poetry are thus also, irrefutably, about politics: "The bulk of [Hebrew] poetry, which is often considered to be exclusively spiritual, is political" (p. 118–119). This statement reflects the fact that, for Herder, the Hebrews were the quintessential *Volk,* with all the multiplicity of meaning he attached to the word.[2] The concept involved religion, nationality, culture, society, and politics, all bound together by a common language. Language not only defined the human being; it was also the primordial instrument of political association.

I wish, for just a moment, to follow Herder in his political exploration of biblical territory. Among other things, he analyzes certain Hebrew inventions that he regards as being of fundamental importance for universal history.

The Solitary Guardian of the Law

The action is set "long ago in a remote corner of the globe" (p. 77). Moses, still surrounded by "savage peoples," has had the unprecedented courage to create a new social order based on the sublime idea of a government of the people—something always desirable but especially so, for Herder, when adapted to a people's own "degree of culture" (p. 117).[3] Such a social organization can be achieved only if "it is the law that reigns, not the lawmaker, and [only if] an independent nation freely accepts that law and willingly abides by it."

Such is the principle of this "theocratic regime," which might also be called "nomocratic" (p. 82). The invisible God is at once "lawmaker, guardian of the law, King." Herder states that the goal of this government is to ensure the happiness and "political prosperity of the people of Jehovah" (p. 101). Mosaic law rests entirely on the law of God, "ratified by the unanimous vote of the people" (p. 118). Since Moses' constant concern is to protect "the liberty of his nation wherever possible" (p. 120), there is no inheritance in the tribe of Levi and no executive or legislative power. All political decisions are taken jointly by the elders of the tribe. This rule is intended to ensure that "there is as little despotic power as possible." Moses imposes no servitude on this "free people" other than "that of the law" (p. 82).

The law was the sole ruler because "the God of Israel had no image" (p. 87). The "books of the law," the ultimate symbol that took the place of any idol, were kept in the holiest part of the tabernacle. The sacred books were "enthroned in the national temple, which is the home of the national God" (p. 118).

Moses was the supreme monotheist. Herder accordingly devoted two chapters to Mosaic institutions and to the man who
succeeded in establishing a law that did not resort to icons and
thus a law that no human royal figure could embody.[4] Enforce-
ment of the law was left entirely to "the sanctuary of the nation." Moses was never tempted to seize power or subject the
people to his own will. He exploded with anger when his trust
was abused in the episode of the golden calf, an idol that "broke
the bonds of the nation."

Moses' work remained incomplete. The perversity of his
people and his own weaknesses prevented him from overseeing
the establishment of his institutions in the land of Canaan. But
what the man who gave Israel the law could not do, "the sages
and poets of Israel did after him" (p. 77).[5]

While Herder sang the praises of the singular *Elohim* and of the
Hebrew language as archetype of all poetic expression and witness to the politics of the prophets, he celebrated with equal
ardor the incommensurable diversity of nations and cultures.
For him, every community and every period of history established its own norms; hence comparison was misplaced. On
what rational basis could one compare the "barbarous, gruff,
and guttural" sounds of the oriental languages with "the silvery
tone of Greek?" (vol. 11, p. 231). Rather than make such
senseless comparisons, it was better to try to understand the
works of a given time and place in terms of their own purpose,
"the ideal of their intention" (vol. 5, p. 492). What point was
there, for example, in criticizing Egyptian funerary sculpture
for lack of animation when its purpose was in fact to portray
dead ancestors in a pose that expressed the absence of life, their
"hands and feet imbued with immobility and death."

Aware of "the deficiencies of generalizations" (vol. 5,
p. 501), Herder hoped to shake the dust off the historical sciences. In order to describe a people or a moment in time, he

tells us, one must first ask "Who am I painting? Who is affected by such a painting in words?" (p. 502). Wary of book
learning, the pastor advises clergymen "to travel in order to
learn tolerance" (vol. 4, p. 477). Nothing can replace the vivid
impressions left by direct contact with other peoples. If one
hopes to understand how far-off nations live, "one must first
sympathize" with them (vol. 5, p. 502). Only then can one
penetrate to the heart of an alien time, region, or history. He
offers his famous recommendation: "Immerse yourself in all
this so as to feel it" (p. 503).[6] There is no other way to express
"the depths of character that are found in every nation"
(p. 502).

What is unique is incomparable. Nothing, therefore, is
more odious to Herder than the "frequent abuses" (vol. 12,
p. 8) of aesthetic comparisons, in which the poetic expressions
and sentiments of a people or period are judged according to
another era's rules of taste. Yet this is what Winckelmann, "the
best historian of ancient art" (vol. 5, p. 491), does when he
looks at Egyptian art with Greek eyes. To write history in this
way, to measure human diversity against a single standard, is
to deprive different peoples of a meaningful place in the march
of history. It is to forget that the Creator did not impose uniformity of taste and feeling on the human race: "Nothing is
more responsive or more varied than the human heart" (vol.
12, p. 8).

The most convincing proof of human diversity, supported
by ties of history and geography, is that "the greatest individuality reigns" (vol. 20, p. 20) in regard to naming "the spiritual and the divine" over the ages. Herder's extremely careful
attention to temporal and regional factors led him to view the
Old Testament as "a collection of oriental writings" expressing
a well-defined cultural type. Although this meant looking at
Scripture as a kind of national folklore, it did not prevent Herder from also considering it an inspired text. While it had to

be conceded that the Hebrew Bible was a composite of many fragments written in different periods, its chapters nevertheless partake of the earliest origin, the "childhood" of the world.[7]

Herder's belief in an irreducible specificity of peoples and periods led him toward cultural relativism, but the resulting conflict with Christian orthodoxy was tempered by a providential vision of human history. His position incorporated two imperatives: every civilization pursues a course characterized by the spirit of its time; yet while no people or period can escape the influence of this *Zeitgeist,* the succession of epochs that constitutes human history is determined by God. In principle, therefore, no one time is superior to any other. Herder generally (but not always) refused to establish a scale of values, a hierarchy of civilizations; instead of *Verbesserung,* or progress with a connotation of amelioration, Herder preferred the notion of *Fortgang,* or growth, permanent change, modeled on nature.[8]

Given this relativist premise, the only way to understand the creative forces of a particular time and place is to approach with empathy the smallest unit of human society that still forms a distinct totality. In travel notes written in Nantes and Paris and appended to a diary Herder kept of his travels in 1769, the young pastor first formulated some of the ideas that he would develop in *Another Philosophy of History* (1774) and *Ideas for the Philosophy of History of Humanity* (1784–1791). His statement flies in the face of the prevailing clerical universalism, which was the universalism of evangelizing Christianity: "No man, no country, no people, no people's history, no state is the equivalent of any other. Thus the true, the beautiful, and the good also are not identical for them" (vol. 4, p. 472).

For Herder, the national question is as much aesthetic and moral as it is religious. In his travel notes he asks if Christianity had not "perhaps destroyed as much as it had contributed" to the many peoples converted over the centuries, often by force. Had Christians sufficiently weighed the dangers of "importing any foreign religion," given the degree to which such importation always threatened the "national character" of a group?[9] Religion always forms an element of a people's national education, an essential part of its outlook. Religious upheaval can therefore destroy a nation's "spiritual riches and characteristics" as well as overturn "venerable prejudices." Herder even goes so far as to question the legitimacy of converting non-Christian peoples. In considering the possibility that conversion is a form of violence, he raises a fundamental question: "Can Christianity justify appropriation, subjugation, and cruelty?" To Herder the answer is obvious. To convert a nation to Christianity by imposing on it a new way of life is to compel it to betray its own values, to lose its own identity, and thus to imperil its spiritual and political integrity. "Did the Americans need a European culture? The Spanish brought them no such thing."

These "thoughts and examples" (p. 469) appended to Herder's 1769 travel diary were further developed in Book 16 of *Ideas,* where Herder advises the "historian of humanity" not to choose one people over another, not to favor only those already crowned by fortune and glory (vol. 14, p. 288). It's a matter of geography: "The Latvian might have become a Greek if he had occupied a different place among the peoples of the world."

Hence no people can claim to be chosen. Even though the Germans *(Deutschen)* occupied the Roman world, that is no reason to regard them as "God's chosen people in Europe" (p. 289) or to assume that they possessed "an innate nobility" in virtue of which "the world belonged to them." There is no reason to believe that other peoples ought to be subject to them, for history shows that the act of subjugating turns conquerors into ignoble barbarians: "The barbarian rules by force; the cultivated conqueror teaches." Thus no nation—neither the ancient

Germans nor the "self-styled people of God" (p. 294)—needs to call itself "chosen."

Everything depends, therefore, on where one people stands relative to another on the stage of history. Nearly all nations have their role to play, but only when "the time is right" (vol. 5, p. 564). The coordination of this cyclic movement in which cultures succeed but do not imitate one another, the direction of this grand drama, is the work of destiny, which calls upon each nation, "when its hour comes, to labor in the vineyard" (p. 563).[10] History thus proceeds in successive waves across continents and generations, forming a "fable with a thousand aspects" (p. 559) whose overall signification cannot be grasped, "at least by the human race." Mortal ears generally remain deaf to this cosmic melody, catching at most a few "dissonances" (p. 560).

This vision of a series of peoples each chosen at its own hour, of perfectly autarchic cultures each bearing the stamp of its own genius and absolute values, leads Herder to consider the possibility of a series of "chosen people."[11] One day, perhaps, a new culture will be born from the quasi-barbarous peoples of the Northwest (vol. 4, p. 402).[12] Not that the Russians are superior to others by nature, but their youth augurs well for the future. If the "spirit of culture" were to inspire the Ukraine, that region might occupy the place of a "new Greece" and awaken to civilization just as "so many minor savage peoples" of Greece had earlier become civilized nations.

A visionary himself, Herder believed that the historian should be "a prophet of the past," a poet whose work is based on an aesthetics of Providence.[13] To find his way in a "labyrinth of a hundred closed gates and a hundred open ones" (vol. 5, p. 560), to bring order to such complexity and diversity, the historian has to remember that the development of mankind is "God's epic" (p. 559). History is controlled by Providence, and it is the historian's task to decipher the signs of this "never-ending drama." Understanding mankind's past thus becomes an art of uncovering the divine order hidden in the Bible. Scripture and history form a pair in which the reality of events demonstrates the truth of the sacred text, which in turn proves the exactitude of knowledge of the past. The science of the Bible and the science of history thus vouch for each other. They correspond in the same way as the image in "a mirror to the person it represents" (vol. 10, p. 140).[14]

When Herder's cultural pluralism ran up against his Christianity, it metamorphosed into a history of religion with undisguised priorities. Surprising aspects of the Romantic sage's work emerge when one follows the alternation in his writings between a very secular ambition to write cultural history respecting national and spiritual diversities and a very Lutheran desire to institute a providential anthropology.[15] Thus, for example, he applies the idea of predestination to peoples, which allows him to ascribe providential significance to each nation's position in space and time. Even more important than the geographical order—civilization evolving from east to west so that it becomes centered in Europe—is the chronological order, according to which the historical importance of each nation is determined by its relation to the Christian calendar. In this hierarchy Christianity clearly reigns supreme.

Herder can move in an instant from fine detail to sweeping generalization. At one moment he takes the generous view that all peoples are equal in merit, each as capable of happiness as the next, each incomparable, incommunicable, and absolute (vol. 14, p. 227), but in the next moment he has adopted a scale of values dominated by white Christian Europeans. Their advantages, the result of favorable geography and temperate climate, supposedly manifest God's choice.

When it comes to the idea of race, Herder vehemently attacks those who "dare give the name *races*" to groups classified by geographical origin or skin color (vol. 13, p. 257). "I see no justification for this terminology." Like Buffon, whose work influenced him, Herder refused to draw inviolate boundaries within the human race. The families of man are linked by bonds "as variable in nature as they are imperceptible" (p. 258). Human varieties are never exclusive; skin colors come in subtle gradations: "In the end there are only shades of difference." Herder tells his reader that "neither the pongo nor the gibbon is your brother, but the [Native] American and the Negro are" (p. 257).[16]

As brothers, moreover, these human beings are not to be killed or exploited. The distinction between man and ape reflects the Christian injunction not to mix the species of living things as conceived by God, each "according to its kind." Thus there can be no familiarity between man and animal, no "fraternizing with apes." Yet this taboo, connected with the Bible's monogenetic premises, did not prevent Herder from speculating that Nature "placed the Black next to the ape" (vol. 14, p. 211), nor from arguing that blacks are "all the more richly endowed for sensual pleasure" because they are without other "nobler gifts" (vol. 13, p. 235). This development of their sexuality, he says, can be seen in their "lips, breasts, and sexual organs," which together are responsible for the unfortunate physical appearance of Africans. For this they are to be pitied rather than despised (p. 236), even though Nature, which "dispossessed" them, did provide them with certain compensations. Herder saw a correlation between these disabilities and the environment, the torrid climate of Africa being too much for human nature. Beauty and order reside "in the middle, between two extremes" (vol. 14, p. 211). That is why reason and humanity achieved their finest form "in the intermediate, temperate zone."

Thus Herder does not attribute the differences between nations to the existence of distinct human "races." His reasoning, which combines historical and geographical analysis, nevertheless implies some kind of "genetic" transmission (vol. 13, p. 258). [17] Like Buffon, Herder believes that there are "varieties in the human species," differences that are "perpetuated from generation to generation." [18] The possibilities and limits of each nation are determined, Herder argues, not only by culture and its indispensable tool, language, but also by constraints of climate and geography. [19] "In other words, the earth is not populated by four or five mutually exclusive races or varieties" (vol. 13, p. 258). To place each people in relation to the others, he proposes "a physical and geographical history of humanity." [20]

Although his catechism prevents him from denying the unity of the human race (vol. 13, pp. 405–406), it does not stop him from regarding certain nations as immobile and excluded from history, not evolving in time or space. Thus, while China deserves credit for bringing culture to its neighbors, Herder expresses aversion for those Chinese "who, in their own corner of the earth, refrained, like the Jews, from mixing with other peoples" (vol. 14, p. 10). Although quick to establish laws and a code of ethics, the Chinese people soon "ended its education, stuck in childhood" (p. 15). A glance at the Chinese language justifies the judgment that "the enormous collection of eighty thousand composite characters" (p. 9) no doubt helped to keep the Chinese in "childish captivity" (p. 11). China is a living fossil, a nation paralyzed by a language that has trapped its people "in an artificial manner of thinking: for is not the language of each country the clay out of which the ideas of its people are formed, preserved, and transmitted?" (p. 13). (Static and childish though it may be, this China, which "drinks hot water" [p. 12] from morning till night, brings "corruption to Europe" by selling it "millions of pounds of tea" [p. 16].)

Herder adopts different points of view depending on whether he is writing the history of humanity, the history of specific nations, or the history of Europe. And if he is capable at times of subjecting all Western-centered attitudes to severe criticism, elsewhere he does not hesitate to employ the "European standard."[21] His international creed made him reject cross-cultural comparison and value hierarchies, but he went on to praise what was unique in each nation. Against the dominant currents of the Enlightenment, he sought to rehabilitate prejudice as an acceptable norm, an often implicit value underlying the spirit, wealth, and autonomy of a cultural system.[22]

His vision of national destiny as totally self-contained even led to a kind of modernism. In this vein he criticized the negative effects of missionary work and attempted to replace the "oriental" narrative of Genesis with an account of the origin of the world better suited to the sensibility and science of his time.[23] His cultural pluralism did not, however, lead him to relativism in religious matters, although the paradoxical tension in his writings did take him some way toward a relativistic position. In one review, for example, he offered an opinion that would seem to rule out interpretation of history on the basis of revealed, absolute truth: "A writer who is a historian of humanity should not have any religion."[24] The strict secularism of this assertion accords well with Herder's praise for human diversity in space and time. Yet in his work advocacy of the equivalence of all nations coexists with the catechism of his childhood. Even when he took openly anticlerical positions he was always working toward conclusions compatible with a Lutheran theology of Providence.

While exploring heterodox approaches, Herder nevertheless clung to at least two convictions: he believed firmly in the unity of the human race, so that when the day comes the Revelation will be made to everyone; and he had absolute faith in Providence as the force that guides universal history.[25] Herder's historical vision was thus Christian through and through, and its coherence was entirely dependent on the illumination of Providence. To remain blind to the meaning that "the will of

Providence" (vol. 14, p. 239) bestowed on nature and humanity was to condemn oneself to utter want of insight or understanding. History would then become "like a spider's web in a corner of the universe" (p. 207), its dark center always beyond reach.

What people, then, did Herder regard as the stars in heaven, the leaven among nations? (vol. 7, p. 370). The idea that all, or "nearly all" (vol. 5, p. 564), peoples are called to contribute to the work of history is somewhat overshadowed by Herder's fleeting conviction that he has discerned which ones are destined to be chosen. While all nations are eligible to join the race for elect status, few make it to the finish line. Providence has its priorities. Indeed, when it comes to choosing among peoples and times, God prefers those few who inhabit "the places where Jewish and Christian revelation received its impetus and from which it was propagated. This is the decisive event. In other regions, independent human reason still lies dormant." (vol. 7, p. 370)

Mythology, liturgy, and high morality can all be found in the Koran, the Zend-Avesta, the books of Brahmanism, and the teachings of Confucius, but nothing in these works can rival "the Revelation in the proper sense of the word." In an earlier version of this paragraph Herder even goes so far as to argue that "our Revelation [therefore] cannot be compared with any other so-called revelation." [26] Thus Herder violated his own ascetic vow not to use the verb *vergleichen,* to compare, in a pejorative sense.

In the fourth and final section of *Ideas* (1791), the last step is taken, leaving Christianity without any rival. Revelation, once given in twin "Jewish and Christian" form (vol. 7, p. 370), is now reduced to the singular. The Christian message embodied in Jesus becomes "the unique design of Providence for our species" (vol. 14, p. 291). The "holy scripture" of the Jews (p. 293), their prayers and moral judgments, are no doubt "sublime writings." But a supreme choice has been made, and "it is good that Providence itself made the decision" (p. 294) in favor of Christianity, because with "the fall of Judea the old walls were toppled."[27]

Thus Herder forgot his concern with impartiality in working out the mechanism of his philosophy of history. He is close to clerical tradition when he identifies the progress of history with the march toward Christianity and finds its meaning in the conversion of the heathen, yet in other respects he departs from that tradition. For his historical faith is not based solely on salvation in the hereafter; it also rests on the meaning of history, whose necessary course is inscribed within events themselves.[28] The course of events describes the intention of divine Providence, which governs everything, nature as well as history (vol. 14, p. 207; vol. 5, p. 559). In analogous fashion, Herder deduces the history of humankind from the development of nature. The same "finger of the Omnipotent" (vol. 13, p. 28) directs both. Thus the sole function of the natural sciences, in conjunction with the humanities, is to reveal the divine order. To that end we must develop every possible technique and discipline, from comparative anatomy to philology. In this way we improve our ability to interpret the multitude of signs "in the labyrinth that is the palace of God" (vol. 5, p. 560) in order to grasp the hidden unity of meaning, even if "total vision" (p. 559) remains beyond mortal reach.

Herder helped to open new avenues for comparative historians of civilization to explore. He was aware of the precariousness of all cultures (vol. 14, p. 147). Epochs, he knew, were fragile things that could "collapse like colossi and bury one another" (vol. 7, p. 369). Once the forces of Christianity appear on the horizon, however, his cultural pluralism collapses.[29] From that point on Herder refuses to tolerate any alien shadow on the stage of universal history. Whether they know it or not, all these peoples from far-off lands sing Scripture's praises. What are the words of these "so-called savages" (vol. 5, p. 566) if not "living commentaries on the Revelation?" It must be so, Herder believes, because Christianity embodies "the most important history of the human world" (p. 567). As the sole bearer of this Revelation, the people of the Christian West relegate all other nations to remaining eternally underage. They disport themselves in a childhood without history, unaware that the future of humankind is at stake.

Chapter 4

The Hebrews and the Sublime

In the autumn of 1845 Joseph-Ernest Renan left the seminary, with the approval of his superiors. Nearly forty years later he remembered that October day when he descended the stairs of Saint-Sulpice "never to climb them in a cassock again." [1] When he left the seminary Renan took his passion for Hebrew with him. He recalled his delight with "the exact philology of M. Le Hir," who taught him Hebrew grammar and introduced him to the comparative study of the Semitic languages (p. 863). He identified with his teacher, a Breton like himself, a man with a character similar to his own, and called him "a scholar and a saint" (p. 857). A model philologist, as rigorous in religion as he was in the study of language, Le Hir settled Renan's future by discovering his vocation: "I was a philologist by instinct" (p. 864). Renan also remembered reading Goethe and Herder at Saint-Sulpice in 1843. Upon discovering German culture he felt as though he were "entering a temple" (vol. 1, p. 438; vol. 2, p. 865). "It was exactly what I was looking for, the combination of a highly religious with a critical spirit. At times I regretted not being Protestant, so that I might be more of a philosopher without ceasing to be a Christian" (vol. 2, pp. 865–866).

However intense Renan's spiritual crisis, his inner struggle between reason and belief, may have been, it was his desire to apply critical philology to the sacred texts of the monotheistic West that finally drove him out of the seminary, or so he believed: "My reasons were all of a philological and critical order.

51

They were not at all metaphysical, political, or moral"
(p. 869).[2] In *The Future of Science: Thoughts of 1848,* published
in 1890, just two years before his death, Renan exalted the
"new faith" that had supplanted his "ruined Catholicism" (vol.
3, p. 715). He was already anticipating his later contributions
to an "empirical science of the spirit" (p. 845). For this science, which he compared to physics and chemistry, he could
find no better name than philology.[3]

In some ways it was Renan's intense interest in Hebrew and
other Semitic languages that estranged him from the Catholic
Church.[4] Thereafter he dreamed of making philology, the secular instrument of his recent emancipation, the supreme arbiter of the human sciences. For Renan as for so many other
scholars in the second half of the nineteenth century, philology
came to embody "the exact science of the things of the spirit"
(p. 847).

Monotheism without Effort

To Hebrew and the people of Genesis Renan attributed a variety of virtues, each accompanied by a corresponding defect.
Because the dazzling light of the Sinai desert tends to create
mirages, Renan perfected his own chiaroscuro, his own way of
perceiving the shadows that give relief to the featureless expanse of the desert. He extolled the glories of Hebrew in am-
bivalent terms, for Hebrew belonged to a bygone era of which
nothing survived but its essence, monotheism. Nor was Renan
the only scholar or theologian to note the striking, not to say
scandalous, fact that an obscure people in a forsaken corner of
Asia had for a long time enjoyed exclusive possession of monotheism (vol. 6, p. 12; vol. 8, pp. 155–156).[5]

Exalted by their unique historical situation between the
Garden of Eden and the Promised Land, the Hebrews, we are
told, were nonetheless rooted in a civilization that was not only

primitive and crude but incapable of evolution. Even more surprising, they did nothing with their treasure, nothing to spread the illumination vouchsafed first to Adam, then to Noah, Abraham, and the prophets. The sublime secret lay buried in sterile ground. The Semites' superintending of monotheism shows how little talent they possessed for propagating the idea or even for using it to combat polytheism. This remained true until the day Christ emerged from their midst.[6] At that point another story began—a story that would continue to call itself "New" even as it sought reassuring genealogical roots.

Renan left Saint-Sulpice to embark on a career as a Hebrew scholar. Indo-European studies being fashionable at the time, the young philologist drew his inspiration from them. Early in his *General History and Comparative System of the Semitic Languages* (1855) Renan announced that he hoped to do "for the Semitic languages what Professor Bopp did for the Indo-European languages" (vol. 8, p. 134).[7] This confluence of the Semitic with the Indo-European or Aryan[8] would shape the future work of the professor of Hebrew of the Collège de France.[9] His whole conceptual scheme is based on these "two rivers" (vol. 2, p. 323), these two linguistic families, which constitute the wellspring of a human civilization in which neither China nor Africa nor Oceania really take part (vol. 8, pp. 580–581 and 586–588). Renan invariably finds one of these "two poles of the movement of humanity" (vol. 2, p. 322), the Aryan, superior to the other, the Semitic. Although they shared "the same cradle" (vol. 8, p. 578), their paths diverged very early on, if not at the very inception then as "twins . . . separated once and for all at the age of four or five." As adults, in any case, they are perfect strangers. The few traces of their common childhood on the heights of the Imaus are recognizable only by philologists, with the aid of fantastic etymologies (pp. 586–587).[10]

Beyond the "family resemblance" (p. 578) that distinguished Aryan and Semite from other races, the two had nothing in common. The great Indo-European family, for example, comprised a multitude of tongues reflecting the distinctive characters of peoples as different as the Indians, the Greeks, the Iranians, and the Germans, whereas the Semitic family consisted of a scant few dialects, no more different from one another than were the members of a single Indo-European group (vol. 8, p. 156).

Furthermore, while the Indo-European languages underwent constant transformation as they differentiated over the ages, the Semitic languages did not change at all. Exempted from time, sheltered from erosion, they were blessed with eternal youth. Fully formed at birth, these languages were incapable of growing old. But, stuck at an infantile stage of development, they were equally incapable of maturity. Static, straitjacketed by its roots (vol. 6, p. 32), Semitic grammar was formed in an instant for all eternity, as was the revelation of monotheism, which one day shone forth "without the slightest effort," "without reflection or reasoning" (vol. 8, pp. 582, 145).

Nothing beckoned on the horizon. The substance of the Semitic languages, Renan tells us, was "metallic" and "pure," like the thought of a unique god who had no image (pp. 137, 145). Trapped in an expanse of time without an exit, the Semitic tongues were strikingly similar and had been "since language first appeared" (p. 137). Their substance thus constituted a kind of "skeleton," and since these languages had remained fundamentally unchanged from the beginning, a philologist might venture to propose a kind of anatomy. According to Renan, every language emerges as it is from the human mind (p. 559). Like a "mold," it then shapes the spirit of the people that uses it (vol. 6, p. 32; vol. 8, pp. 157 and 514). The Semitic language is distinguished for its capacity to convey what is immutable. This unalterability, regarded as an objective linguistic fact, of course matches the image of the Hebrew people as unchangeable, allegedly impervious to history and uncompromising in their faith. Once again we find the old idea that there is a necessary link between the structure of a language and the spirit it represents—or, to put it another way, the idea that language mirrors the soul of a people (see Chapter 1).

But this legendary vision of Israel also depicts a community composed essentially of expert conservators whose sole activity, as pious as it is sterile, is to preserve their religious patrimony. It is a way of bestowing a permanent, ahistorical identity on the Hebrew people in order to perpetuate both aspects of its traditional role vis-à-vis Christianity. On the one hand the Hebrews are assigned a "sublime mission": it was to them that monotheism was revealed, albeit in some sense without their knowledge.[11] On the other hand, the distinction of having been chosen for this role is diminished by the charge that the Hebrews exhibited "such unfortunate fidelity"[12] to their original faith that they failed to recognize Christianity as "the definitive religion" (vol. 4, p. 362).[13]

For Renan, then, the theory of language is not simply akin to but identical with the theory of religion. The languages in which monotheism was first formulated were carved, he says, in impervious, hence unalterable, "bedrock" (vol. 8, p. 541). These languages, with their invisible vowels, have a hard core, intolerant and tyrannical, whose message can be summed up by its persistent repetition of the formula "the Lord is God" (p. 149).

The Indo-European languages, implicated in the movement of history and destined to proliferate, were quite different, and it was from their study that the science of linguistics arose. No such science could ever have emerged from "exclusive study of the Semitic languages" (p. 137), which are as changeless as the landscape in which they were born: "The desert is monotheistic, sublime in its immense uniformity" (p. 147). In such a place it is easy to go astray, to follow trails that lead nowhere. Neither space nor time leaves a trace, and such emptiness hinders creativity. No divine image or temple breathes life into this territory. Religion had to make do with minimal paraphernalia, nothing but "a movable ark" containing a few pieces of parchment (1859, p. 426; vol. 6, pp. 56–57).[14] Impervious to history, the "languages of steel" (vol. 8, p. 542) prevailed in these surroundings and shaped the spirit of the Semites.[15] "Peoples dedicated to immobility" (p. 162, and vol. 3, p. 861), their nature was symptomatic of the tenacity of their opinions; their languages were no more malleable than their mentality, which lacked a driving force to set it in motion.[16] At a time—the nineteenth century—when everything was measured by its historical potential and teleological contribution to evolution and progress, the monotheistic miracle was linked to Semitic stagnation.

Renan thus credited the Semites with a "minimum of religion" (1859, p. 253), a monotheism that was "the fruit of a race that has few religious needs" but was equipped with a "superior instinct" for religion (vol. 8, p. 145). Looked at more closely, this monotheism, this pure essence of the religious, amounted to "a set of negative injunctions" (vol. 6, p. 56). The nomadic Semite was at once "the most religious and the least religious of men." Maximum and minimum coincided. Although the language of the Semites suffered from serious grammatical and syntactic deficiencies, it was nevertheless replete with its sublime origins, imbued with the memory of the first awakening of human consciousness. Both the language and the religion stood, so to speak, at degree zero, yet even this minimal amplitude was enough to permit the emergence of the "monotheistic instinct" (1859, p.426).

It was impossible to break free of these languages, with their metallic structures, just as it was impossible to throw off the rigors of monotheism, with its dry spirit "devoid of all flexibility" (1859, p. 423). Since the spirit of a people is inextricably intertwined with its linguistic system, their "very thought is profoundly monotheistic" (1859, p. 431). More precisely, since language for Renan was first of all a question of race, a "mold" as decisive in its influence as was the shape of the cranium for adepts of physical anthropology, the Semitic languages became "the organs of a monotheistic race" (vol. 8, p. 97; 1859, p. 216).

There was, in Renan's view, an inevitable correlation between the categories of a language and the categories of the spirit that shaped that language. Language was intimately bound up with the system of constraints underlying the religious tradition and with a way of being in the world that grew out of articulating the phenomena of the visible and invisible universe (vol. 8, p. 96). Everyday perceptions, as well as mythological, juridical, ethical, political, military, and artistic structures were shaped by the same factors.

Portraits of Races

Renan attributed all the positive and negative characteristics of a community to "race," a term that occurs frequently in his writing. The notion of race, he says, has both valid and invalid uses. In presenting what he calls "portraits of races," he knows that he must "prevent misunderstandings" and even "grave errors" (1859, pp. 444–445). In order to "clarify the value of the term," Renan several times expounds its meaning at length. [17] Although nineteenth-century scholars never achieved consensus on a definition, the concept of race, polysemic though it remained, was so widely used that it achieved normative status. Many authors wrote as though the history and future of mankind could be cast in terms of a hierarchy determined by race.

Excerpts from texts that Renan published between 1855 and

the end of his life illustrate his raciological view of languages
and peoples. It is hard to attach any single interpretation to
these passages. To do so one would have to focus exclusively on
the hierarchical aspect of the concept, always present in Renan's thought, while excluding other aspects. To force Renan's
texts to speak with a single voice is not necessarily to do them
a service.[18] A different approach makes more sense. The criteria
that Renan uses to classify peoples reflect the political tensions
of his time. What I want to show is how, using these criteria,
he is able to juggle with the vague concept of race, attaching
to it a meaning sufficiently precise for his own scholarly purposes.

What did Renan's "portraits of races" look like?[19] Humanity,
he tells us, was long ago divided into families, each different
from the others, each with its virtues and faults. "The fact of
race was then paramount and governed all aspects of human
relations" (1859, p. 445). This very remote time in ancient
history cannot be understood without a concept of racial dis-
tinctions, "the secret of all the events in the history of humanity" (p. 446). Originally, then, races were "physiological
facts," but gradually their importance waned. Owing to great
conquests and to the spread of religions such as Buddhism,
Christianity, and Islam, the era of racial determination gave
way to an age of "historical facts." "Language thus virtually
supplanted race in distinguishing between human groups, or,
to put it another way, the meaning of the word 'race' changed.
Race became a matter of language, religion, laws, and customs
more than of blood" (vol. 6, p. 32).

Renan immediately tempers this assertion by insisting that
the "hereditary qualities" of blood help to perpetuate institutions and "habits of education." Although, for Renan, "races
are durable frameworks" (1859, pp. 447–448), things have
reached the stage where they are "no longer anything more
than intellectual and moral molds" on which physical kinship

has "almost" no influence. The philologist even goes so far as to propose that the term "linguistic races" be substituted for "anthropological races" (vol. 8, p. 1224). Consider, for example, Muslim Africa and Asia: these regions of the world are perfectly representative of the "Semitic spirit" (1859, p. 448) even though their "pure Semite" population is insignificant. In other regions, a Brahman, a Russian, and a Swede might exhibit no physical resemblance and yet "certainly belong to the same race" (vol. 8, p. 576). Conversely, Aryans and Semites might exhibit "no essential difference" in physical type and yet belong to "two [distinct] races" by virtue of their "intellectual aptitudes and moral instincts" (p. 577).[20] Following the same line of argument, according to which physical factors, though not altogether negligible, nevertheless play a less important role than "linguistic race," Renan remarks that "the Turk who is a devout Muslim is in our day a far truer Semite than the Israelite who has become French or, more precisely, European" (1859, p. 448).

In one sense, Renan continues, the declining importance of "anthropological race" represents "spiritual progress" (p. 449). When the Apostle Paul expressed the wish that one day there might no longer be "Jew nor Gentile, Greek nor Barbarian," he was voicing the hope that "men might forget their earthly origins in order to subsist in brotherhood born of their divine nature."

Yet nothing, Renan concludes, can eliminate the "diversity" that has existed since the inception of humanity.[21] Notwithstanding various strictures, "the idea of race remains the principal explanation of the past." From the standpoint of cultural anthropology Renan invites his readers to agree that "history is the great *criterium* of races" (pp. 444–445). Here his historical vision is perfectly static, however. The civilized peoples—the Aryans and Semites who sprang from the cradle of Western civilization—never existed in "the savage state" (vol. 8,

p. 581). Nor is there a single example of a savage people that has attained to the state of civilization: "To imagine a savage race speaking a Semitic or Indo-European language is a contradictory fiction" (vol. 8, p. 581).

To verify the truth of this assertion, Renan tells us, we have only to compare the races, as depicted in his "portraits," with "the historic roles of the peoples themselves" (1859, p. 444). In other words, the major contributions made by those peoples that Renan regards as the promoters of civilization prove the inferiority of all other peoples. Conversely, the immobility of these inferior races, which are incapable of evolution, attests to the grandeur of progress in the West.

This distinction, between those equal by virtue of their civilization and all the rest, who are their inferiors, reappeared in a more immediate contemporary and political context.[22] When Renan spoke out on the issue of what constitutes a nation,he insisted even more emphatically that "the zoological origins of humanity" (vol. 1, p. 897) considerably predate the first appearance of culture and language. Race, once of paramount importance, has since lost its decisiveness. Humans, being neither rodents nor felines, "have no right to go around the world probing into craniums and then grabbing people by the throat and telling them, 'You are our blood; you belong to us'" (p. 898).

Although Renan elsewhere attempts to demonstrate the pertinence of the concept of "linguistic races" (vol. 8, p. 1224), even they have no meaning in the present.[23] He is writing in Europe, where civilization has come together to found modern nations based on the exclusion of everything hostile to human liberty. Races may still have a role to play, but not in Europe. Science must recognize them for what they are: unbreachable dikes erected by nature between the civilizations of the West and the rest of humanity. In "European nations" (vol. 1, p. 455), however, race—whether defined in terms of blood or language—has no further role to play and therefore no place. "The political importance that people attach to language comes from the fact that it is seen as a sign of race. Nothing could be further from the truth. . . . Languages are historical formations, which tell us little about the blood of those who speak them and which in any case cannot fetter human liberty. . . . Let us cling firmly to this fundamental principle, that man is a reasonable and moral being before being rooted in one language or another, before being a member of one race or another, before belonging to one culture or another" (vol. 1, p. 900).[24]

Not even this famous statement is wholly free of ambiguity. A glance at other texts is enough to show that Renan ascribed "human liberty" primarily to the "superior races" (vol. 1, p. 390). He no longer takes the trouble to distinguish between "linguistic races" and "anthropological races" or between "ancestors according to language" and "ancestors according to blood" because his center of interest has once again shifted. His attention is no longer focused on the science of ancient humanity or the theory of the nation but on the politics of late-nineteenth-century colonialism. His prose also changes; he adopts a completely different style. Instead of allusive or evocative metaphors we find the peremptory assertion of a triumphal and unambiguous philosophy. Along with the two speeches cited earlier, the passages we are about to examine from *Intellectual and Moral Reform* (1871) must be understood in the context of Franco-German controversies that flared up during and after the Franco-Prussian War of 1870–71. Renan claims to subscribe to the new "providential order of humanity" (vol. 1, p. 390): "There is nothing shocking about the conquest of a nation of inferior race by a superior race, which occupies the country in order to govern it."

Renan rejects the conquest of a race by its "equal," but anything that contributes to "the regeneration of the inferior or bastardized races by the superior races" is to be recommended. For Renan, "superior" humanity is identified with Europe.[25] As the repository of "the common idea of civilization" (vol. 1, p. 455), Europe is also the only place where equality is a civil right: "Of course we reject the equality of human individuals and the equality of races as fallacies: the higher elements of humanity should dominate the lower elements. Human society is a multistory edifice, in which gentleness and goodness (which man is required to display even toward animals) must prevail, but not equality. However, the European nations as history has made them are peers in a great senate, each of whose members is inviolable" (vol. 1, p. 455).

Renan's aim here is to identify and to uphold the hierarchical, "Providential" order of peoples, an order dictated by the "natural" characteristics of the races (vol. 1, p. 390). Just as some peoples play a more important role than others in the theater of history, some contribute a great deal to the development of civilization while others contribute little or nothing. The well-being of all depends on recognition of this order, which the history of humanity must follow. "Let each [people] do that for which it is made, and all will go well" (p. 391).

The key to world political and economic harmony is colonization, which is supposed to achieve this providential result. Nature, by endowing each people with natural qualities and assigning to each race a historic role, "has made a race of workers, the Chinese, marvelously dexterous in handiwork yet with virtually no sense of honor; a race of tillers, the Negro; [and] a race of masters and soldiers, the European" (p. 390).

At the end of his life, in the preface to *The Future of Science* (1848–1849), Renan stated that he had not formulated "a sufficiently clear idea of racial inequality" (vol. 3, p. 723). Over the past forty years so much progress had been made in history, philology, and comparative religion that it was now possible to state the "general laws" (p. 724) of the civilizing process. Bolstered by recent scientific discoveries, Renan is thus able to say: "The inequality of races is a proven fact.[26] Each human family's claim to more or less honorable mention in the history of progress has been in large part determined" (p. 724). Within the family of civilized races, Renan carefully apportions credit between Aryans and Semites. The professor of Hebrew at the Collège de France reverts constantly to these "two rivers" (vol. 2, p. 323) from which all thinking humanity has flowed. Let us follow him for a while as he constructs his great Aryan-Semitic myth on the ruins of his lost Christianity. Let us follow him as he explores the two strands of his ancestry, as he seeks to restore to the West the memory of its linguistic forebears, the Indo-Europeans, and to tell the tale of Israel's Semitic origins, from which Jesus liberated its religion.

A Grandiose Trap

"Arid and grandiose" (vol. 7, p. 339)—Renan's words for the simplicity of monotheism. The divine secret in all its intransigence lies couched in the Semitic languages that convey its harsh message. For proof, consider the Semitic verb, incapable of being conjugated for tense and mood (vol. 6, p. 35; vol. 8, pp. 157–158). Instead of inflections there are a scant "few parasitic monosyllables" (vol. 8, p. 158). Devoid of syntax, lacking conjunctions, incapable of managing the inversion that allows the Aryan sentence to "preserve the natural order of ideas without impinging on the definition of grammatical relations" (p. 160), the Semitic languages are powerless to formulate, hence to conceive, multiplicity (p. 146). Even though God, *Elohim,* is plural, it takes a verb in the singular (vol. 6, p. 48). Moreover, the articulation of the many facets of nature is foreign to Semitic imagery.

Yet if an excessively simple language renders Semites incapable of abstraction, metaphysics, and creative intellectual activity in general (vol. 8, pp. 96 and 157), other forms of expression are open to them. The sensual nature of the Semitic tongues is well suited to the singularly affective character of Semitic poetry. The only art of which the Semitic peoples are masters, moreover, is "music, the subjective art *par excellence*" (p. 152). Melody comes into being instantaneously, without effort. Rhythm leaves no perceptible trace yet lives on in the body as blind or unreflective memory.

What can be represented in music is as indeterminate as the notation of vowels in Hebrew. We are not surprised to discover that this musical language occupies a special place in Renan's portrait of Semitic monotheistic idioms as sensuous tongues powerless to conceive the world in its complexity, incapable of articulating in abstract terms concepts born of rational effort.

By contrast, Aryans, thanks to their rich grammar and syntax, understand the animation of nature in its multiplicity (1859, p. 257). Blessed with wit, they can play with the secrets of the universe, revealed in the words of language. Mythology has discovered the existence of "a vast play on words" (vol. 7, p. 742). Citing recent work by Max Müller, Renan reads the plurality of natural phenomena in the names of the gods. Behind each word root lurks "a hidden god" (1859, p. 429). The difference between the Semitic and the Indo-European peoples is striking not only in language but also in religion: in effect, Aryan religion turns out to be "an echo of nature" (vol. 8, p. 581). For Renan this observation offers one more opportunity to point out that, whereas the Semite finds monotheism perfectly natural, the Indo-European does not. When certain Indo-European peoples finally do succumb to Jewish, Christian, or Muslim preaching (unlike India, which has "remained mythological to the present day"), it is only with "extreme embarrassment" (pp. 581–582) that they convert to monotheism.

We are a long way from those Semitic provinces ruled by a

"God formed of the fusion of nameless gods" (vol. 6, p. 65). Instead of praying indiscriminately to a single being, as the Semites did, Aryans worshiped specialized divinities (p. 50). This wealth, this complexity of spirit was responsible for the earlier inferiority of the Aryans' culture. A polyvalent understanding of nature is a bewildering thing, and for a time the Aryans lost their bearings.

The Semites never experienced such a threat (1859, p. 444; vol. 8, p. 587). Their paradoxical glory was of a different kind. If initially they enjoyed the advantage, sheltered as they were from the grandeurs and delusions of polytheism, ultimately they suffered the consequences (1859, p. 444; vol. 6, p. 65; vol. 8, p. 146). Their great privilege closed on them like a trap. The same rich spiritual underpinnings that predisposed the Aryans to the delusions of mythology and the proliferation of gods later led them to discover metaphysics, physics, and the scientific principle. Semitic monotheism, which had been the cause of such rapid development, just as quickly became "an obstacle to human progress" (1859, p. 444; vol. 8, p. 587).

Renan then points out how the multiplicity of pagan myths and gods also implies "freedom of thought, a probing spirit" (vol. 8, p. 148). These are at the heart of such richly imaginative societies, which leave "the boundaries of God, humanity, and the universe floating in an indeterminate haze." Childlike, these peoples freely conceive "multiplicity in the universe" (p. 150), and therefore speak the languages of polytheism. When the age of maturity comes, these same peoples invent the formulas of science.[27]

The early glory of the Semitic race ultimately worked against it: first among the peoples of the world to recognize a unique divinity, it fulfilled its destiny "in its very first days" (p. 146). Like those with "less fertile natures who, after a blessed childhood, achieve only a mediocre virility" (p. 156), the Semitic nations fell victim to a fundamental flaw: they were incapable of "perfectibility." [28] While Semitic monotheism may envision a solitary and perfect God, it nevertheless remains stuck at an infantile stage of human development. The monovalent religious spirit, like the languages that articulate it, is inherently static.

Renan concedes that the Semitic race has rendered an immense service to the human race (1859, p. 432), but an "entirely negative service," decidedly inferior to the Indo-European contribution, which is nothing less than "the *substratum* of all civilization."

Perhaps we can now understand two aspects of the work of this historian of the chosen people: his praise of their negative contribution, and his insistence on the dual nature of the Hebrew. Charged with an essential mission in the midst of the desert, the Hebrew, Renan tells us, was incapable of the slightest reflection. Paradoxically, this inaptitude for reflection is the consequence of a potential that flares up briefly and just as suddenly cools when it must find its bearings in time and space. Although the Hebrew did indeed recognize that God is one, that truth descended upon him: he had no responsibility in the matter. His monotheism was in no sense a product of his mind.

"One does not invent monotheism" (vol. 7, p. 87). It is "the result of special gifts" (1859, p. 216) distributed "exclusively" to the Jewish people. No borrowing from Egypt, no philosophical rumination could have given rise to this luminous revelation, which one day burst forth "without any effort" (vol. 8, p. 582; 1859, pp. 215, 221–223, and 229).

If the Semite is therefore supremely gifted in religion but unfit for science, the reason has to do with his inability to conceptualize multiplicity, which for Renan is the hallmark of the ability to comprehend reality. [29] The Semitic intelligence suffers the same handicap: it can neither symbolize (vol. 3, p. 1141, n. 128) nor idealize (vol. 8, p. 162). In the realm of discourse it therefore cannot go beyond the proverb parable, or Bible verse (pp. 150, 160, 479–480). The epic inspiration, the ability to weave together several systems of divine imagery, is wholly beyond the Semite's grasp (1859, p. 438).

Thus for Renan the Semite's "monotheistic instinct" (p. 426) is merely an instance of a more general principle, "the absence of fecundity in imagination and language."[30] The same principle explains why Semites are without fancy and utterly humorless: they "almost completely lack the faculty of laughter" (vol. 8, p. 152). One final paradox must be noted, however: Semitic intransigence is no sure protection against polytheism, because even the most insignificant painted or sculpted image is enough to plunge the race into idolatry (1859, p. 425). Only the extreme rigor of the Hebrew lawgiver prevented the Semites from succumbing to the "perpetual seduction" of polytheism (p. 237).

Some Semites, perhaps, were seduced by the gaudy spectacle of the multifarious visible world. Renan is willing to concede the point, but it scarcely arouses his interest. In the first place, no Semite of the primitive era ever succumbed: the race was then purified of "all infidelity" (vol. 8, p. 147). Furthermore, "Semitic paganism" is never anything more than a mask for "primitive monotheism" (1859, p. 272). The proof lies in the fact that every Semitic word for god contains the generic *El*. Thus while Renan concedes that some Semitic peoples did practice religions that appear to be polytheistic, they did not do so in response to the same natural forces that animate the Aryan gods and universe. The Semitic gods are merely emanations, divine variations on a single theme. All the names of *Baal* or *Bel* are signs that refer back to an "undivided" divine power (pp. 258–262). Only the philologist deceived by some epithet of the supreme God (p. 269) can think that the Semites worshipped multiple deities.[31]

Like the course on "Mohammedanism" that Edgar Quinet

(1803–1875) gave at the Collège de France in 1845, Renan's portraits of Semitic daily life reflect the rigors of the desert.[32] No political philosophy, no civil or military bureaucracy could arise in so desolate a landscape (vol. 8, pp. 153–154). The only strategy that could be practiced in such featureless terrain was entrenchment in the sand. Thus the conquests made by the Semitic religion of Islam were the result of proselytizing more than of military art (pp. 170, 175–176).

This monotheistic civilization was nomadic at heart. A movable ark had to be invented for its invisible god. Semitic society was little more than a tribe, without "political or judicial institutions" (p. 153). Whereas Quinet maintained that Jehovah established "a social desert around himself,"[33] Renan sought to demonstrate this impoverishment by appealing once more to the nature of the Hebrew language, for so long deprived of even the most rudimentary grammar: a "beautiful language [that] bears no trace of deliberate lawmaking" (vol. 8, p. 259).

Renan, it should be clear by now, was adept at ringing the changes on his fundamental theme, that the civilized world was divided between two antithetical principles. Perhaps it is worth mentioning one final demonstration of this point: among the polytheistic Aryans of primitive times, Renan tells us, the family unit observed a "strict monogamy" (vol. 6, pp. 34–35), whereas the monotheistic Semites were polygamous. Of course this polygamy was also inimical "to the development of all that we call society" (vol. 8, p. 152).

The Stock and the Flower

Renan pursued his Semitic studies against the background of the newly emerged Indo-European sciences, which had a profound impact on his understanding. Renan's image of Semitic monotheism is reflected in an Aryan mirror: he incorporates—

and in a sense dissolves—the Semitic race into a history from
which the Aryan outlook emerges triumphant. This Aryan outlook, originally polytheistic, later found embodiment in the
"moderate" monotheism of Christianity.[34]

Renan's examination of Semitic monotheism also takes into
account contemporary responses to a range of values associated
with Indo-European polytheism. Numerous passages in his
writings shed light on the Aryan-Semitic dialogue of the nineteenth century because Renan, like the Romantics, knew how
to express the concerns that underlay his writing. In a notebook he observes: "Everything I have done is a mere shining
sepulcher to my lost faith."[35] His *Souvenirs* reflected his moti-
vations as much as did the metaphors that breathed life into
his work as a philologist and historian of the origins of Christianity.

Because the Aryan-Semitic schema was at once logically coherent and hierarchical, Renan, like Pictet and so many other
subsequent writers, was forced to try to wrest Christianity
from the clutches of Semitic monotheism. In notes that he took
while researching the *Life of Jesus*, Renan unambiguously stated
a theme that he would later reproduce in countless variations:
"The thought of Jesus stemmed from a high conception of divinity, which, owing nothing to Judaism, was in its entirety a
creation of his great soul. . . . Fundamentally there was nothing Jewish about Jesus."[36]

This rescue operation, designed to save Jesus from Judaism,
proceeded along several avenues. Christianity, Renan tells us,
was "less purely Semitic" (1859, p. 422) than Judaism or Islam; it became "the least monotheistic" of the three revealed
religions. If Christianity thus "completely transcended the
limits of the Semitic spirit" (p. 440), it did so because it
adopted the spirit of the peoples it converted. Renan's inaugural lecture at the Collège de France took a similar tack: "The
victory of Christianity was not secure until it completely broke

out of its Jewish shell and again became what it had been in the exalted consciousness of its founder, a creation free from the narrow bonds of the Semitic spirit" (vol. 2, p. 332).

Western Christendom thus had an enigmatic ancestry, Aryan in its linguistic system and Semitic in its religious faith. To resolve this ambiguity, Renan cast his lot with those who, having delivered Jesus from Judaism, "aryanized" Christ: "Originally Jewish to the core, Christianity over time rid itself of nearly everything it took from the race, so that those who consider Christianity to be the Aryan religion par excellence are in many respects correct" (vol. 5, p. 1142). Islam constituted a stage in this process of aryanization: "The continuation of Judaism was not Christianity but Islam." [37]

Not only was Christianity not a continuation of Judaism, it actually contradicted the Jewish religion, which had provided the early church with "merely the yeast that initiated fermentation" (vol. 1, p. 240). If the Hebrews performed a "negative service," Islam "did more harm than good to the human race." Hence Renan could not refrain from approving those scholars who maintained that "Christianity improved itself by moving farther and farther away from Judaism and seeing to it that the genius of the Indo-European race triumphed within its bosom" (vol. 1, p. 240).

In order to aryanize even more fully the birthplace of civilization, Renan followed a historiographic tradition that provided a coherent geography for this project. He proposed that Eden had been located in Kashmir, in the ancient kingdom of Oudyana, which means "garden" (vol. 8, pp. 566–567).[38] It is interesting to note in this connection the belief of at least some educated Europeans, as reflected in a June 7, 1855, letter from Richard Wagner to Franz Liszt:[39] "Thanks to modern scientific research, it has been shown that pure, unadulterated Christianity is nothing other than a branch of the venerable Buddhist religion." [40]

Having saved Jesus from Judaism, Renan awarded him the lush green land of Galilee, which contrasted sharply with the sterile desert of dogmatic Judea. "In this earthly paradise" (vol. 4, p. 178) Jesus was welcomed and understood. Here, too, shone the first glimmer of human progress. Eighteen centuries later, it was impossible not to recognize the universal, eternal character of the Christian religion, in many respects "the definitive religion" (vol. 4, p. 362; vol. 1, pp. 272ff).

In this geography of the imagination we note the usual contrast between Aryan and Semite, between northern Palestine and Jerusalem. Because landscape influences dialect and thus shapes a people's spirit (vol. 8, pp. 95–96), locale and climate together establish a sharp boundary between Galilee and Judea, between paradise and desert. The barrier is also spiritual, and it is as unbreachable as the gulf between the races always is for Renan. There is an "abyss between Semite and Arian."[41] That is why "the North alone created Christianity" (vol. 4, p. 125). On the other side of the divide lay the scene of the crucifixion. Judea is "the saddest country in the world," a region encrusted with a monotheism hostile to Jesus. The land of Judea exemplifies the characteristics of extreme monotheism, whereas Galilee, joyful and tolerant by comparison, embodies a "less harshly monotheistic" spirit.

This combining of two opposite poles to form a complete universe can also be found in Greece.[42] What two cities could be more different than Sparta and Athens, so close and yet always "rival sisters"? The same could be said of the Hebrew people in Palestine, divided between Jerusalem, "the true homeland of obstinate Judaism," and Galilee, "a green, shady, delightful country" in which Jesus felt at home.[43]

In the introduction to the *Life of Jesus* Renan stresses the importance of his travels in Palestine to the writing of his book.[44] "The striking accord between texts and places and the marvelous harmony of the evangelical ideal with its natural setting were a revelation to me. I beheld before my eyes a fifth Gospel, torn but still legible" (vol. 4, p. 80).

This "fifth Gospel" was immediately legible to Renan, for whom sacred geography dispelled historical time. The flora and fauna of Galilee still flourished, while Judea remained as arid as ever. In the mild month of April 1861, "the flowers of Galilee were unrivaled in their beauty," and "Jesus loved flowers, from which he drew his most delightful lessons."[45] Renan attached great importance to capturing the atmosphere of the Holy Land in metaphorical flights. He evoked the colors and smells of the seasons for his readers, whom he invited to share in his enchanted discovery of plants, lakes, and mountains.

For Renan, the nature and climate of a place were important determinants of the psychology of its inhabitants. Henriette Psichari understood her grandfather's passion. "As for individuals, Renan deliberately assumed that they were identical to those who lived in the past. When he saw one woman on her way to the fountain and another sitting in her doorway, eighteen centuries evaporated, and he beheld Martha and Mary and Mary Magdalene, barefoot and veiled."[46] Renan wanted his Jesus to be in harmony with his surroundings and to that end gave him character traits that he saw in the course of his travels. "He was by no means exempt from the faults of his coreligionists. To this day insulting in controversy. Exchanging insults." Landscape and psychology, geography and history—all served the author of the *Life of Jesus* in his aim of contrasting the "naturalism of the North" with "the abstractions of Jerusalem."[47] The difference between the two zones of Western spirituality thus lay at the source of Christianity. Renan paired Aryan and Semite in order to bring out the contrast between them.

A metaphor drawn from the plant kingdom neatly encapsulates Renan's evolutionary thinking: "The Bible thus bore fruits that were not its own. Judaism was the stock on which the Aryan race produced its flower" (vol. 5, p. 1143). Thus a metaphor takes the place of a conceptual statement in Renan's approach.[48] He uses his metaphorical system to generate analogies and series of images. We have already encountered a number of such analogies, based on appearance.

Renan was convinced that we are "haunted by our origins" (vol. 6, p. 66) and that the Christian who seeks to understand his origins must come to terms with Hebrew (vol. 1, p. 909). The Jews may have introduced humanity to "a religion substantially superior" (vol. 7, p. 823) to that of the Aryans, but the Vedas remain "the key to our origins, the primitive revelation of our ancestors, to which our conversion to Jewish ideas should not make us indifferent."

These problematic filiations, according to which the Christian is at once the heir of an alien "monotheistic race" (1859, p. 216) and the descendant of ancestors who practiced a multifarious polytheism, leave several questions unanswered: How could one be Semitic and monotheistic in religion and Aryan in language, if religion and language were inextricably intertwined in a spiritual form that in theory had to be either one or the other? How could this dual heritage be explained? How could one live with it? The tension is explicit in Renan's text: "Alone among the peoples of the East, Israel enjoyed the privilege of writing for the entire world. Admirable as the poetry of the Vedas is, this anthology of the first songs of the race to which we belong will never replace the Psalms in the expression of our religious feelings, even though those Psalms are the work of a race so different from our own" (vol. 8, p. 258; vol. 7, p. 80).

This explanation by way of chiasmus also crops up in a slightly different form. Renan says that polytheistic Greece is to the Indo-Europeans what monotheistic Israel is to the Semites (1859, p. 216). Thus Socrates, in opposing Athens, played a role comparable to Jesus' in opposing Jerusalem; we recall that Renan earlier paired Galilee and Jerusalem with Athens and Sparta. And we come back once more to the Vedas: Sanskrit is the counterpart of Hebrew, because each tongue is the "key," the "repository of the secrets" of its corresponding linguistic and intellectual family (vol. 8, p. 238).

Clearly, the Christian may feel Aryan, but his heart is Semitic, pulsing with a force that is at once intrinsic and alien. His ancestor, who belongs to "a race so different from our own," is the monotheistic, Semitic Hebrew. A foreigner from a distant land, this Hebrew is the author of the Psalms and hence at the heart of the Christian identity. Thus for Renan, the Christian can affirm his heritage only by absorbing this alien yet strangely intimate presence.

Within the linguistic pairing of Sanskrit and Hebrew, the Aryan distinguishes himself through "a system of metaphysics," whereas the Semite achieves immortality with "a sweet, sensual poem" (vol. 3, p. 863). Onomatopoeia dominates in the Semitic languages, whereas Sanskrit possesses certain words that seem always to have had a "conceptual meaning" only (vol. 8, p. 74). Christianity emerged from the pairing of these two dramatically unequal languages. Ultimately the abstract reason of the Aryans achieved supremacy over the religious exaltation of the Semites.

"The Cause of Christianity"

"A scholar and a saint" (vol. 2, p. 857), Renan's description of Le Hir, the Hebrew teacher at Saint-Sulpice with whom the young seminarian identified, could equally well be applied to himself. A verbal magician and piper of enchanting melodies, an artist and poet who was also an eminent scholar, Renan no doubt saw his life's work as revealing unsuspected affinities between religion and science.[49] Because he understood all too well that the Catholic Church looked askance on any such marriage, he chose not to follow in the footsteps of his admired predecessors: "Herder was the German writer I knew best. His very broad views enchanted me, and it was with great sorrow that I had to say, 'Ah! Would that I could think such things and still remain a minister, a Christian preacher, like Herder!'" (vol. 2, p. 875).[50]

We have yet to discuss how Herder integrated his estrangement from the Church into his work. Although he issued stinging denunciations of belief in the supernatural, superstition, dogma, and other "shocking nonsense" (vol. 5, p. 1146), and although he proclaimed the decline of Judaism and of certain forms of Christianity (vol. 5, p. 1146; vol. 6, pp. 1516ff), he did not wish for the disappearance of religion—which in his eyes, as far as the civilized peoples were concerned, meant Christianity (vol. 4, p. 363; vol. 5, p. 1145). Although he advocated a clear separation between "ecclesiastical society" and "civil society" (vol. 5, p. 1148) he was convinced that religion was an institution necessary for the "nourishment of the soul" and the harmonious equilibrium of the "normal man" (vol. 1, p. 280), for it must never be forgotten that "the infinite overwhelms and obsesses us" (p. 168).

Thus Renan was not at all worried about Europe's religious future, convinced as he was that "the nineteenth century will not, as has so often been said, witness the end of the religion of Jesus" (p. 171).[51] Belief in the supernatural would soon disappear from the world, but not religion, which was as necessary to humanity as poetry and "as eternal as love" (p. 170). The reason was simple: "Man will never be content with a finite destiny." Superstition must therefore not be confused with religion, and Christian dogma must not be confused with the religious principle proclaimed by Jesus.[52] Only that principle was destined to develop indefinitely. The religion of the future would thus necessarily take the form of "liberal Christianity, [which] alone is eternal and universal" (p. 273).[53]

Renan was nothing if not prolific in his assertions. He did not shrink from taking contradictory positions, because he believed in the overall coherence of his convictions. On one point, however, he was uncompromising: Christian dogma was based on revelation and thus on miracle, which was incompatible with science. "Struggle is therefore inevitable" between Christianity and science (vol. 5, p. 1144). What, then, did Renan mean by "the religion of Jesus" (vol. 4, pp. 362–364), which he claimed was definitive? What did he mean by "Christianity," if Christianity was just another word for religion?

Christianity, born of "the rupture with Judaism" (vol. 5, p. 1142) and embodying European memory, was elaborated by "people of our race." Not even the "freethinker" (p. 1145) could deny that Christianity was the religion of the European nations, although as an individual he was free to make his way as he pleased in total independence. History, for its part, was steeped in Christian meaning. It was no more possible to deny this than to exclude oneself from civilization: "Christianity is, as a matter of fact, the religion of the civilized peoples. Every nation admits this in one way or another, depending on its level of intellectual culture" (p. 1145).

Thus it was the Christian tradition that supplied the moral fabric common to all civilized nations. It is a mistake to think that Renan wished to reduce the influence of "the sum of religion that still remains in this world" (vol. 1, p. 168). Nor does Renan believe that a revolution, whatever its nature, can destroy the religious bonds that unify the modern nations into one great family. Their solidarity is based, Renan tells us, on intellectual and moral values at the root of which "shines the name of Jesus" (vol. 4, p. 364). If philosophy began with Socrates and the scientific spirit with Aristotle, it was Jesus who founded "the absolute religion" (p. 363) by establishing once and for all the very concept of the "pure creed": "In this sense we are all Christians, even if we differ over nearly every point of Christian tradition" (p. 364).

Christianity is therefore the only possible source of a common European memory, of an ethical and aesthetic tradition rooted in the archives of civilization. The religion of Jesus moreover "contains the secret of the future" (vol. 1, p. 168). Renan also emphasizes another crucial point in his concept of Christianity: unlike the Church theologians, Jesus did not establish any dogma. Instead he brought a "new spirit" into the world (vol. 4, p. 362). His teachings were "so undogmatic" that he never thought of "writing them down or having them written down."[54] Hence there is no reason for Christianity, understood in this way, to come into conflict with the scientific spirit. It is a part of that spirit: "In this sense, learned colleagues, by following a purely scientific course I believe I am serving the cause of the true religion and, I would even add, the cause of Christianity" (vol. 1, p. 170).

"Future" and "progress": therein lay the secret of the religion of Jesus. Europe thus contributed to the glory of the Christian ideal, all the more so because the moral teachings of the founder of Christianity "contain the seed of all progress" (p. 170). Science and religion are henceforth paired in the providential dynamic of the only plausible future for Western civilization.[55]

In an analysis of Renan's work published in the year of his death, Maurice Vernes (1845–1923) paid homage to Renan by pointing out how "he restored a *possible* Jesus . . . a *possible* Christianity."[56] Instead of throwing stones at him, Vernes suggests, intelligent Christians "ought to thank him."

Renan chose the course of Christian rationalism: he purified religion of miracles, superstitions, and other pious nonsense that in his eyes amounted to a negation of the religion of Christ. By ascribing to Jesus an exceptional place in history, a key role in the evolution of civilized humanity, he sought to use philology to create an irrefutable scientific basis for Christology.[57] In so doing he hoped to establish a firm and objective link between Christian truth, shorn of all superstitious nonsense, and the positive truth that nineteenth-century science dreamed of discovering. He combined the reason of the Enlightenment with the truth of the Gospel. Using this dual frame of reference he wrote a history of humanity whose unabashed guiding principle was the march of civilization. Civilization was identified with the single notion of progress, but its memory comprised two strands, one Aryan, the other Semitic.

The final chapter of his *History of the People of Israel,* completed on October 24, 1891, barely a year before his death, contains two images: "a desiccated trunk" (vol, 6, p. 1513), symbolizing what Judaism had become, and a "fruitful branch," representing Christianity. These metaphors supplanted those found in his earlier *Marcus Aurelius,* where the "Aryan branch" came between the Christian "flower" and the "first Jewish stalk" (vol. 5, p. 1145) or "stock" (p. 1143).[58] Only the dynamic history of the "Aryan race" could account for the providential metamorphosis of Christianity. Perhaps Renan felt such an attachment to Christianity because he identified with his Celtic and Germanic ancestors, who had made their own contributions to the development of the religion.[59] His eulogy for Ernest Havet,[60] delivered on Christmas Eve of 1889, is unambiguous: "All that is best in Christianity we have placed there, and that is why Christianity has such a powerful hold on our hearts, that is why it must not be destroyed. Christianity is in a sense our work. . . . We are Christianity, and what we love in it is ourselves. Our cold green fountains, our oak forests, our cliffs have had a part in making it" (vol. 2, p. 1129). Pressing the point, Renan adds that such Christian ideals as charity and love of one's fellow man "come more from our ancestors, pagans perhaps, than from the selfish David or the exterminator Jehu."

Aryan and Semite were thus caught up in a genealogical drama for which Renan and many of his contemporaries, in various ways, sought a providential and Christian resolution. For Renan, the Aryans were the linguistic ancestors and the Semites the unwitting founders of modern religion, primordial twins kept apart by time and space. The characteristics he ascribed to each group stand in sharp contrast. The Aryan trait always dominates, contradicts, encompasses, or complements the corresponding Semitic trait. Some of these binary pairs have already been touched on: abstract metaphysics versus sensuous poetry, scientific reason versus religious feeling, philosophy versus music, family versus tribe, political organization with all that it implies versus desert nomadism.

These characterizations were closely related to Renan's evolutionist view of history.[61] The religion of Jesus had to be aryanized, freed from its congenital Semitic shortcomings, in order to participate in progress. To that end the Hebrews were consigned to an ahistorical existence. The people of Israel with their static theology play an atemporal role, which is to highlight Christianity's temporal progress and evolutionary development. The "monotheistic race" (1859, p. 216) is frozen in time. Wedded to its linguistic system, Israel is equally trapped in the terms of a sacred history according to which its destiny is simply to be what it already is, the chosen people of Providence.

From Renan to Richard Simon

Once upon a time there was a great biblical scholar, a man whom Renan described as "an astonishing genius [who] with one stroke placed religious scholarship on a foundation that has never been shaken."[62] In praising this scholar, Renan deplored that Bossuet and his successors had seen to it that his name would be forgotten for generations. Richard Simon was more than the author of the *Critical History of the Old Testament*.[63] Unafraid to go "into the field" to explore the ethnography and customs of the Jews, Simon sampled the religious attitudes of Jewish communities in his own day, studied local variations in Jewish customs, and observed the variety of Jewish rituals in Italy, Germany, Spain, and Turkey.[64] He sought to comprehend the Jewish religion in a variety of ways, including translating Rabbi Leon of Modena's *Ceremonies and Customs Observed Today among the Jews* from the Italian.[65] In the preface to that work Simon wrote: "Since the Christian religion derives from Judaism, I have no doubt that reading this little book can shed much light on the New Testament, owing to its similarity to and connection with the Old. Since the men who composed the New Testament were Jews, it is impossible to explain without reference to Judaism. Some of our ceremonies come from the Jews. The doctrine is almost the same. As for ethics, the Ten Commandments are theirs as well as ours. Even Purgatory . . ."[66]

Though always mindful of his Christian objectives, the Oratorian nevertheless catalogued texts and customs that might shed light on the Hebrew religion of the Old Testament. He also sought to understand Jewish customs in terms of Jewish religious categories. From his critical reflections on the Old Testament and ethnographic investigations of Jewish ceremonies Simon derived a vision of the Jewish people that did not limit them to the role of theological witnesses or conservators of ancient values.

In what was supposed to be a petrified religion Simon discovered a living population. His attentive gaze brought Jewish communities to life and showed how the religion had adapted to different times and places. For Simon the Jewish people was not merely a passive witness to history. He saw that, while the Jews had a history before the birth of Christ, they had not remained frozen in time. Like other peoples, the Jews were subject to the laws of history.[67]

Jacques Le Brun gives a good account of this aspect of Simon's work, which fostered an understanding of "Jews not as theological witnesses, eternal symbols of divine punishment, but as a living historical people organized into communities and possessing a civilization. He also compared their ceremonies with those of Christians."[68] Simon's project, however, was ahead of his time, and he was not permitted to carry it out. It would have required a comparative historical and ethnographic study of the various forms taken by revealed religion and monotheism in the West.

Simon offered critical answers to new questions. Without abandoning the Church's interpretation of Scripture, he helped to forge new bonds between faith and scholarship, religion and science, revealed truth and historical observation.[69] Two centuries later, Renan, mindful of Simon's pioneering role, used the new Indo-European studies to write his very Christian history of the people of Israel.

Chapter 5

The Danger of Ambiguity

Born in Dessau in 1823, the same year as Renan, Friedrich Max Müller settled in Oxford at the age of twenty-six. When he died an illustrious scholar in 1900, Queen Victoria sent a message of condolence to his widow. Fascinated by everything to do with Sanskrit, Max Müller attended Franz Bopp's lectures in Berlin in 1844 and the following year went to Paris to hear Eugène Burnouf.[1] In 1849 he won the Volney Prize for a treatise in comparative philology examining the relation between the Indo-European languages and the origins of civilization.[2] Like Renan, he reached a wide audience with his many books.[3] For more than forty years both scholars worked with the concept of race, with the categories Aryan and Semite; only at the end of their lives did they remind their readers of the need for caution in dealing with such ideas. It was not until after the events of 1870 that both men suddenly realized the dangerous racist implications of the science they had done so much to develop and make fashionable: comparative philology.[4]

Despite what they had in common, the two men were very different. Max Müller, for example, did not share Renan's view that the Semites possessed a specific instinct for religion. He launched a polemic against the idea of "Semitic monotheism" which began by summarizing the views of his French colleague.[5]

Renan, as we have seen, considered the Hebrews as existing outside space and time, forever condemned by their language to a destiny without a future. They were not, he argued, the inventors of monotheism in the sense in which the Greeks were the inventors of philosophy. Because he rejected out of hand the notion that the Semites were more talented or intelligent than other peoples, he could not bear to credit them with the invention of monotheism. Since the concept of a single God could not, according to Renan, be the result of deliberate effort or religious philosophizing, he attributed it to a religious instinct similar to the instinct responsible for the development of the Semitic languages (pp. 474–475).

Arguing against this view, Max Müller pointed out that true instincts are invariable: "Fishes never fly, and cats never catch frogs." If there were such a thing as a religious instinct, it would have been permanent. But this was not the case. Jewish monotheism had at times gone into eclipse, such as when the Hebrews erected altars to foreign gods. Moreover, if monotheism was a peculiarly Semitic aptitude, how could authentic Aryans such as the Greeks and Romans convert to become disciples of a monotheistic Christ? Max Müller preferred his own theory of the origins of the divine. He founded a school of comparative mythology that, although much criticized, attracted many adherents up to the middle of the twentieth century.[6]

Divine Appellations

Max Müller showed how the idea of God had affected man since the most ancient times. In the beginning, at the time of the creation, was what he called a "primitive revelation."[7] When God breathed life into man, he also endowed him with an "intuition" of the divine. This primitive intuition, a consequence of creation alone, "was in itself neither monotheistic nor polytheistic," although it could become one or the other "according to the expression which it took in the languages of man." Various names were given to this primordial spark; thus we may assume that human languages diverged from the moment the intuition of the divine was implanted in primitive man. The link between divinity and language opened a vast field of inquiry for the new science of language that Max Müller hoped to master. As he put it: "The history of religion is, in one sense, a history of language."[8]

If more than one language exists, God must have many names. The biblical truth must remain inviolate: in the beginning God revealed himself to "the ancestors of the whole human race" in the same way.[9] Accept this principle, Max Müller tells his readers, and "everything that follows becomes intelligible."

By analyzing individual words, Max Müller was able to solve many important problems. He is immediately struck by the thought that if the Semitic languages are poorer than those of the Aryan family, this impoverishment may have been an advantage. Because the root of a Semitic word is easy to identify, its substance is at once visible and transparent. Each word retains its concrete meaning, thereby preventing confusion. In a Semitic dialect the words for "the tent of heaven" or "the dawn" (p. 488) have such a distinct objective sense that those who used them as divine names could never have been misled, could never have confounded the luminous sky with God or the dawn with a goddess. The Semitic vocabulary applies only to visible, material realities; it does not register the supernatural.

Aryan words are very different. The root, swamped by prefixes, suffixes, and derivatives, is less easy to discern, to the point where the substantive sense of the word is blurred; words cease to be appellations. Aryan words are probably freer than Semitic words. They have greater charm, and their seductive richness no doubt encourages the creative imagination. But that is precisely where confusion and error may creep in. The Semite did not have to resist the seduction of words or the resulting mythology: "The names with which he invoked the Deity did not trick him by their equivocal character" (p. 498).

The Semites could, however, sink into idolatry when an adjective was transformed into a noun. They could then confound a singular divine quality with the subject to which it applied. The various names of a single being could then metamorphose into denominations of multiple beings. When the Jews "fell into idolatry," however, they felt guilty because they still clung to the "uncontradicted" idea of one God.

For the Aryans, language was a daily peril, a ubiquitous snare. Consider the sun.[10] Its proud radiance, though a source of life, was also terrifying. Since the Aryan denomination lacked the transparency of the Semitic term, and since there were different appellations for different aspects of this star, names became traps; *nomina* became *numina*. A simple source of light thus became the supreme being, the world's judgmental eye, and the universal creative power. As its personal faculties were developed, the solar star acquired the capacity to heal, and to pardon simply by forgetting what it alone could see. When the root of the word was lost entirely, a primordial intuition became a solar god. As a Sanskritist, Max Müller was able to trace the shift from the perception of a natural phenomenon to the figure of a mythic god in the Vedic hymns.

In the Aryan tongues every word represented a potential myth. A name or even an attribute could give shape to a god. Eos was the word for dawn before becoming the goddess of the rising sun. Zeus, Jupiter, and the Sanskrit Dyaus, all names for the supreme god, were once common terms for the daylit sky. The Aryan languages, and in particular Sanskrit, were rich in metaphor and therefore fertile soil for myths. The moment a metaphor supplanted a word and obscured its concrete root, the danger of myth reared its head. In his eighth lecture, devoted to the subject of metaphor, Max Müller wrote: "Whenever a word is used metaphorically and without a clear notion of the stages by which it passed from its original to its metaphorical meaning, there is danger of mythology. When the steps of the process are forgotten and replaced by artificial ones, we have mythology, or, if I may put it this way, a disease of language." [11]

This forgetting of the metaphorical process and hasty personification of natural phenomena are both consequences of the opacity of Aryan words, whose enigmatic roots encourage fantasy. Language thus afflicted becomes a source of myth. [12] Max Müller insisted on the need to distinguish between religion and mythology, the "healthy body" and the "sick body." Even among the ancients, the evident ubiquity of myth presupposed a "healthy religion." How could the Greeks have imagined plural gods without a prior intuition of divinity? Idolatry requires the application of a divine attribute to something that "has no right to it." Thus the assertion that "the sun is god" depends on a prior idea of the divine.

Although mythology therefore invaded the religion of the ancients and nearly killed it, "nevertheless, we can always glimpse the primary shoot around which the lush, poisonous phraseology of myth wraps itself, and without which it could not enjoy even the parasitic existence that has so wrongly been regarded as an independent form of life." [13]

No mythology can uproot this primary shoot. It is "what we call religion," and Max Müller knew it to be engraved in the human heart, no matter how savage. He therefore set out to explore the many religions of humanity, driven by inner faith in "an infinitely wise, infinitely powerful, eternal Being, ruler of the world." To that end he combined the "science of language" with the "science of religion." [14]

In addition to monotheism and polytheism, Max Müller proposed a third category: henotheism, which he believed to be the unique original form of all religion. [15] If polytheism worshiped "many deities which together form one divine polity, under the control of one supreme god," and monotheism venerated only one God while denying all others, henotheism denoted that primitive state of religion in which "each god, while he is being invoked, shares in all the attributes of the supreme being."[16]

The god worshiped in this way was the elect deity of the moment, but a moment later might be succeeded by another. Underlying this system in flux was the monist divine intuition, which Max Müller linked to a revelation. With the same original intuition in each case reflected in the mirror of a particular people and in the words of a specific language, the divine could assume a variety of forms.

While Renan "polytheized" Christianity by aryanizing it, and Pictet, as we shall see, "monotheized" the Aryans in order to make them better Christians, Max Müller opposed the theory of a Semitic monotheistic instinct by arguing that monotheism was the common property of all humanity, because intuition of the divine had been given to man at the time of the Creation. This primary intuition, which he called henotheism, was then shaped by the nature of language into a variety of religions, some monotheistic, others polytheistic. Thus, for example, the limpid poverty of the Hebrew vocabulary prevented the Jews from succumbing to the charms and perils of a multiplicity of divine names. By contrast, since myth depends for its existence on the ambiguities of language and the confusion of images, the Aryans for a long time suffered from their mythology, "that scourge of antiquity [which] is in reality a disease of language."[17]

A Strategic Science

The reader of Max Müller must confront his intellectual choices. His theological presuppositions determined his approach to linguistics and religious history.[18] These positions are evident in his debate with Charles Darwin (1809–1882) as well as in his explanation of why philology should be considered a natural science.[19] We encounter them again when he discusses the Christian basis of comparative studies. His aim is to promote use of the comparative method in the brand new science of religion, and at times his pronouncements take on a militant tone.

Max Müller pursued his inquiry by tracking individual words. His desire to dig down to "the roots of human speech" was of great importance to him, all the more so because that was where "the essential elements of all religions" lay.[20] In his view, the development of language was closely related to manifestations of "the intuitive idea of God." In every person, religion and mother tongue are intimately related (pp. xxxiii–xxxiv).

Max Müller's conception of linguistic science can be seen in his debate with Darwin, who assumed that animals and humans shared a rudimentary linguistic capacity.[21] Max Müller, by contrast, insisted on the importance of "the radical period" when the "roots" of language, "our most venerable title to the faculty of reason," first developed (p. 347). An unbreachable barrier thereafter divided humans from animals. During this period "certain fundamental elements, very simple but highly human, emerged within language, veritable phonetic cells usually known as *roots*. The old question of the origin of language was therefore replaced, as it is here, by the new question of the origin of these roots."[22]

Max Müller categorically opposed the application to linguistics of Darwinian theories, according to which man is "the descendant of a mute animal."[23] There was no evidence for the belief that bird songs or animal cries could evolve into articulated language. Even if a bird like the parrot could imitate the human voice, that was not what Max Müller meant by language. The emergence of language roots marked a clear dividing line between man and beast, "an abyss that can never be bridged." [24]

Max Müller saw the "science of language," also known as comparative philology, as occupying a strategic position among the sciences of his day. Its role was to study that which distinguished human beings from other animals. Its method, he argued, should be the same as that of botany, geology, and anatomy. In these disciplines comparison and classification had already proved their worth by making rapid progress possible. Whereas the ancients saw the material world as mere illusion, or at best as a theater for the random play of atoms, natural science revealed laws that made it possible to understand how nature was organized. It could now be taken for granted that "there is in the animal kingdom the same order and design that we find in the infinite variety of plants or in any other realm of nature. . . . There is a chain that proceeds by imperceptible degrees from the lowliest infusoria to man, the king of creation; all things reflect a single creative thought and are the work of an infinitely wise God." [25]

Evaluating the sciences then in the throes of revolution, Max Müller expressed surprise that comparative philology did not rank with botany, geology, and anatomy. He attributed this omission to a misunderstanding, which he set out to dispel. Human knowledge, he pointed out, fell into two parts depending on the object of study: "the natural sciences and the historical sciences, the former dealing with the works of God, the latter with the works of man." [26] The study of language was not classed as a natural science because people were "misled by the term comparative philology," which reminded them of "philology in the usual sense of the word." The older philology, which dealt with classical and Oriental languages and literatures, was indeed a historical science. But for Max Müller the goal was to make language itself—"language and not languages"—an object of scientific investigation. By studying the "origin, nature, and laws" of linguistics one could explore the link between the development of thought and the invention of language.

Max Müller took a resolutely optimistic view of the contribution that the new methods of the natural sciences could make to history. Although Renan differed with the Oxford don on a variety of issues, he shared this euphoric outlook. In a letter to Marcellin Berthelot published in October 1863 he praised recent successes in comparative philology and mythology: "Concerning our race in particular, we now have, thanks to the subtle researches of Kuhn, Max Müller, Pictet, and Bréal, a clearer view of the primitive Aryans . . . prior to their dispersion than we have of certain contemporary societies in Africa and Central Asia." [27]

Scholars in general were convinced that comparative methods would reveal, if not the origins of mankind, at least a period much earlier than that accessible through even the most ancient written documents. Renan was keen to tell Berthelot what rank he thought the new sciences ought to occupy: "Comparative philology and mythology take us back well beyond historical texts, almost to the beginnings of human consciousness. If the sciences are ordered by chronology, then these two disciplines should rank between history and geology" (p. 636).

Max Müller was unambiguous about the orientation of his research: "We are entering into a new sphere of knowledge, in which the individual is subordinate to the general and facts are subordinate to laws. We find thought, order, and design scattered throughout nature, and we see the dark chaos of matter illuminated by the reflection of the divine spirit." [28]

These words suggest a scientific program consonant with a theological effort to reveal the divine in all things. Max Müller hoped to apply this program to the new philology. Using taxonomic and comparative methods, the new discipline, like other natural sciences, should strive to reveal the providential unity underlying the variegated world of appearances. This providential order had been inscribed in nature at the beginning of time, and it was the task of comparative philology and mythology to find its traces in myths and religions, among which Christianity of course occupied a unique position.

The theological intentions that governed Max Müller's approach explain why the comparative method sometimes functioned in his work as a way of replacing or even annihilating historical time.[29] He did not hide the apologist aspect of his desire to show that all religions were based on the same intuition, the same revelation, the same providential truth. The Christian side of his work became militant in his recommendations to missionaries. Max Müller deplored the tactlessness they sometimes exhibited in their dealings with pagans: "The man who is born blind is to be pitied, not berated. . . . To prove that our religion is the only true one it surely is not necessary to maintain that all other forms of belief are a fabric of errors."[30] Indeed, missionaries should find it advantageous to stress the resemblances among various beliefs and creeds rather than accentuate their differences. Such a pragmatic approach, inspired by the new "science of religion," should make it easier "to look out more anxiously for any common ground, any spark of the true light that may still be revived, any altar that may be dedicated afresh to the true God."[31]

If Max Müller fought hard for recognition of "the legitimate place of the religions of those called uncivilized,"[32] the logic of his argument simultaneously assured the immense superiority of Christianity "over all other religions."[33] This conviction even became a cornerstone of his scientific approach: "The Science of Religion will for the first time assign to Christianity its right place among the religions of the world; it will show for the first time what was meant by the fullness of time; it will restore to the whole history of the world, in its unconscious

progress towards Christianity, its true and sacred character." [34]
A good disciple of Augustine, Max Müller was fond of citing
his remark that Christianity was simply the name of "the true
religion," a religion that was already known to the ancients and
indeed had been around "since the beginning of the human
race." [35]

Programmatically as well as practically, some of the nineteenth-century "sciences of religion" were thus sacred sciences.
Heirs to a still vital past, they were animated by the great
providential design that was impressed on humanity in the first
days of creation.

In affirming the permanence of human intuition of the divine, Max Müller was arguing for the unity of the human race
and for the spiritual identity of its members in all times and
places. Wherever mortals uttered articulate sounds, Max
Müller recognized the "spark" of Christianity.

Chapter 6

The Monotheism of the Aryas

The year 1859, which saw the publication of Darwin's *Origin of Species,* was also the year in which a monumental "essay on linguistic paleontology" appeared under the title *Les origines indo-européennes ou les Aryas primitifs* (Indo-European Origins, or the Primitive Aryas). Its author, Adolphe Pictet (1799–1875), belonged to one of the leading families of Calvinist Geneva. It was because of Pictet's publications that Bopp in 1838 decided to include the Celtic languages in his work on comparative grammar. [1]

Pictet, a man of many passions, ranged widely in his work: mathematics, literature, natural history, philosophy, ballistics, and aesthetics, which he taught briefly at the University of Geneva. [2] His teachers included some of the leading minds of Romantic Europe. In Paris in the fall of 1820, he conceived an enthusiasm for Victor Cousin (1792–1867), whose course had just been suspended by the Commission de l'Instruction Publique. [3] Together with Cousin, the apostle of eclecticism, Pictet dreamed of founding a *Revue de philosophie,* but the proposed journal was never to see the light of day. Before leaving for Germany, a country that Cousin greatly admired, Pictet took courses with François Guizot (1787–1874) at the Sorbonne, met Benjamin Constant (1767–1830), and probably began the study of Sanskrit with A. Wilhelm von Schlegel (1767–1845), who instilled in him a love for India.

It was during the winter of 1821–22 that Pictet made his pilgrimage to Germany, the land of poets and philosophers.

There he met Goethe (1749–1832), Schelling (1775–1854), Schleiermacher (1768–1834), and Hegel (1770–1831). In letters to his father he recounted his private conversations with Hegel and described the philosopher's "obscure and confused" style of teaching, which he had "all the difficulty in the world" following.[4]

The next year Pictet was on the move again, first to London, then to Edinburgh, where he took an interest in the ancient language of the Druids. While delving into the controversy over the authenticity of the poems of Ossian, he came upon an Irish grammar that kindled his passion for the Celtic dialects of Great Britain. He immediately recognized their kinship with the classical languages and Sanskrit, and these observations culminated in a series of lectures given at the Institut de France in 1836 and published in Paris the following year.[5] Jakob Grimm (1785–1863) called upon his services as a Celtic expert in 1855 to decipher a book on black magic written in a corrupt Gallic dialect.[6]

During his time in Geneva Pictet took part in a bizarre escapade with three tourists: George Sand (1804–1876), Franz Liszt (1811–1886), and Liszt's friend the countess Marie d'Agoult (1805–1876).[7] Upon his return from Chamonix he wrote a memoir of the event, or a "fantastic tale" as he called it, which certain of his colleagues sternly disapproved.[8]

Last but not least, Pictet was also a lieutenant-colonel of artillery, one of those academics who practice the art of war before distinguishing themselves in science. Throughout his life he sustained a passionate interest in ballistics. In 1827 he built the first "Pictet fuse," and in 1848 he published an *Essay on the Properties and Tactics of Artillery Fuses*.[9] Later he perfected a percussion detonator, which he had a great deal of trouble persuading anyone to buy, though he solicited all the governments of Europe. Napoleon III's ministry of the navy mulled over the possibility for some time before finally disappointing

Pictet in 1857, and it was not until 1858 that Austria finally
acquired the secret of the percussion fuse, which was to serve
"until 1868 as a hollow-charge detonator for field and moun-
tain pieces." [10]

Bones and Words

Of all those who sang the praises of primitive Aryanism, Pictet
was undoubtedly the most lyrical. His desire to bring knowledge of Indo-European civilization to the broad public is evident in every page of his trilogy, the first edition of which won
the Volney Prize for 1863. [11] In these volumes Pictet does not
burden himself with such technical matters as verb forms or
endings. His method is that of a linguistic ethnographer in
search of words capable of bringing the primitive Aryas back
to life. [12] What did the Aryas pass on to their descendants—
among whom Pictet counts himself—other than their language? Language is the only way to rescue the Aryas from the
obscurity of the centuries. Pictet therefore embarks on a jour-
ney of "linguistic paleontology," tracking the destiny of words.
His mission: to revive Indo-European memories in a Christian
Europe that is in search of an even brighter future.

The structure of the work reveals Pictet's method as well as
his interest in ethnography and geography, in the natural history, material civilization, sociology, and intellectual, moral,
and religious life of the "primitive Aryas." He begins by de-
scribing the providential role the Aryas were called upon to
play from the beginning. As a favored race, blessed with "innate beauty" and "gifts of intelligence," they were destined to
conquer the world. Pictet's book begins with a statement of
"the nature and purpose of the work":

> In an epoch predating all historical records, cloaked in the
> darkness of time, a race destined by Providence one day to
> dominate the globe slowly came of age in what was to be the

training ground for its brilliant future. Outstripping all others in innate beauty and gifts of intelligence, nurtured by a grand but harsh natural setting that was generous but not lavish with its treasures, this race was destined from the first to conquer. . . . It was therefore quick to develop gifts of the mind, for planning, and energy, for execution. Once initial difficulties were overcome, it enjoyed the tranquil well-being of a patriarchal existence.

While thus jubilantly growing in numbers and in prosperity, this fertile race forged itself a powerful tool, a language admirable for its richness, vigor, harmony, and perfection of form; a language that spontaneously reflected all the race's impressions, its tenderest emotions, its most naive admirations, but also its yearning for a higher world; a language full of images and intuitive ideas, bearing the seeds of future riches, of a magnificent outpouring of the noblest poetry and profoundest thought (vol. 1, pp. 7–8).

In these same introductory pages the author also defined his project and described his method. Taking as his model new techniques for analyzing fossils, he hoped to give voice to the vestiges of the Arian vocabulary as other scientists reconstituted the life of an animal—its feeding habits and other behavior—from a few bones: "For words last as long as bones, and just as a tooth implicitly contains parts of an animal's history, a single word can lead to the whole series of ideas associated with its formation. Thus the name *linguistic paleontology* is ideally suited to the science we have in mind" (p. 14).

Pictet's goal, like that of Renan and Max Müller, was to allow a "people unknown to any tradition" (pp. 12–13) to be "in some sense revealed by philological science." Though aware of the difficulties that lay ahead, Pictet assured his readers that, with the aid of words taken from Arian tongues, he would guide them "sure-footedly" (p. 16) to the "birthplace of the world's most powerful race, the very race to which we belong."

The first Aryas, prior to the diaspora, were "essentially a

pastoral people" (vol. 3, pp. 410 and 519).[13] They were not nomads, however, and lived in "fixed" dwellings. Everything known about them suggests that they were "an eminently intelligent and moral race" (p. 269). Is it possible to believe that people who ultimately brought such intensity to intellectual and religious life started from the lowly estate of either having no religion or wallowing in the abyss of an obscure polytheism (pp. 411 and 483)? Pictet attempts to answer this question by "monotheizing" the Aryas as much as he can. Although he concedes that ultimately their religion "consisted in a poetic polytheism" (p. 410), the words of their language—that repository of primitive imagery—reveal the existence of a "primitive monotheism" (p. 483) among the Aryas.

If polytheism developed gradually, there must at one time have been an inferior stage, "a simpler religion" (p. 411). Since the primitive Aryas were so gifted, why might this religion not have been "a monotheism, not rational and reflective but instinctive and more or less vague?" This intuition is bolstered by further observations. After discussing such Arian practices as prayer, libations, and sacrifices, Pictet notes that there is no evidence for an institutionalized priesthood or for "temples and idols consecrated to worship" (p. 533).

Pictet then attempts to provide philological justification for the notion of "primitive monotheism" by examining Indo-European words for the divine (p. 486). The Sanskrit word *deva* attracts his attention. Can a word exist without a prior meaning? If *deva* is attested, then so is the implicit sense of "superior Being" (pp. 412–413). Now, it happens that this word has an exemplary history. It was carried over from Sanskrit into Greek and from there into Latin, "to be transmitted to Christianity, replacing the Jehovah of the Hebrews."

Pictet also supplies proof by contradiction. If the first Aryas had been polytheists worshiping nature in all its multiplicity, their language would have preserved traces, but none exist. "It

must therefore be granted that there was a time when polytheism did not yet exist yet language was already formed"
(pp. 482–483).

Although Pictet pointed out the specificity of Hebrew
monotheism (pp. 485–487) long before Father Schmidt
(1868–1954), he also invited readers to survey primitive deities from the Supreme Being of the Guaranis of Brazil to the
Great Spirit of the Algonquins. Ultimately the palm for savage
monotheism goes to the Indians of Peru, who worshiped an
invisible Being that could not be represented by any idol
(pp. 484–485).[14]

Taking his inspiration from Max Müller, Pictet built the
notion of primitive monotheism around the celestial God of
the Sanskrit texts. If the Aryas later fell into polytheism, it was
because they felt the need to "explain the multiplicity of natural phenomena" (p. 487). Perception of these phenomena gave
rise to new words, out of which grew a host of gods. Shrouded
in mystery, the Aryas' idea of God remained "in an embryonic
state," and their rudimentary monotheism lacked rigor. Pictet
readily concedes all this, all the more readily as it is hard to
explain why, having once known the truth, the Aryas should
have abandoned it for error. Weak and vacillating as their monotheistic vocation no doubt was, it was nevertheless providential; it would fall to Christianity to nurture the seed first
planted by the Aryas.

Among the Aryas certain tribes remained more faithful to
memories of the past. Pictet was thinking here of the tradition
of the monotheistic Zoroaster paralleling the biblical Moses.
The point is not without importance, for it suggests the existence, in an Aryan country, of an "ancient monotheism of
which all memory has not been lost" (p. 492). Pictet was thus
able to demonstrate to nineteenth-century Christians the invention of an early form of monotheism outside the Semitic
tradition. The adaptability of the Iranian magus served histo-

riography in other ways as well. In 1932, for example, the great Indianist Sylvain Lévi (1863–1935) wrote: "Persia, moreover, had profited from the Encylopedists' polemics against the Christian church. The sonorous and mysterious name of Zoroaster, exalted by the classical tradition, made it possible to erect a rival to Moses. Persia vied with the Hebrews for the glory of having set forth the first sublime law." [15]

Pictet's readers were not wrong to see his *Origins* as a kind of Aryan ethnology. As he journeys through the land of the first Indo-Europeans, Pictet communicates his enthusiasm by abolishing all distance between himself and his remote ancestors. Words exert a magical power, encouraging him to sublimate time and space. Not only Renan but also Quatrefages (1810–1892), a naturalist and anthropologist, was powerfully moved, to the point where they believed that they had a better idea of this resurrected prehistoric society "than of many contemporary societies." [16] Pictet's admirers felt comfortingly close to the pre-diaspora Aryas, all the more so in that they shared a sense of forbidding distance between themselves and the African and Asiatic societies of their own day.

A Young Student by the Name of Saussure

Ferdinand de Saussure (1857–1913) was fifteen years old when he sent Pictet his first essays. Though aware that he was "always keen to make systems before studying things in detail," he nevertheless expressed the hope that the old master would "look through these elucubrations." [17] When a posthumous edition of Pictet's *Origines indo-européennes* appeared five years later, Saussure, during the month of April 1878, published in the *Journal de Genève* three articles on the life and work of the man who was his first intellectual guide. [18]

After a sympathetic account of the many interests of the man he characterized as "a scholar and poet," Saussure proceeded to an examination of Pictet's major work, which he said took the reader "to the threshold" of the origin of language and "of the human races themselves." [19] He raised a number of critical points. Is it really legitimate, Saussure asked, to posit "the fact of a people-race" even though the nature of such an entity may be destined to remain forever mysterious? Can one really rely on the comparative method when that method makes so much of "the irresistible logic of the linguistic fact"? [20] To be sure, one could now reconstruct the original form of an Indo-European word, trace its variations, and even "say which syllable the accent falls on." But none of this proves that Bactria was the homeland of the Aryas. Although "the dictionary of the Indo-European language" had long since been compiled, many problems still remained. The transparency of Pictet's work, the answers that emerged from his "very simple and very brilliant" account, concealed many difficult questions.

Among these questions one loomed as paramount: How did the diaspora of the Aryas come to pass? Were they firmly wedded to one language before departing their homeland, or must one assume that they spoke several dialects from the beginning: "In a word, what family tree must be drawn?" In contrast to those who supposed that the family of Indo-European languages all descended from a common ancestor, Pictet assumed a "diversity of language within geographical and political unity." [21] By positing a diversity of dialects from the outset, Pictet was able to argue that a prehistoric political solidarity bound the Indo-European peoples together, and it was on that basis that he consolidated the future of the Indo-European heritage.

In the final article of the series, Saussure considered the notion of a "mother language," possibly Sanskrit, which Pictet shared with other linguists of his generation. No one could fail to notice Pictet's "paternal solicitude," his inability to deny

anything to "his beloved Aryas". [22] Among the traits with
which he endowed them were advanced agriculture, "law of
property," and "love of work." He also loved them "too much"
to deny them happiness, prosperity, and the blessings of a primordial monotheism. But as the twenty-one-year-old Saussure
pointed out to his readers, "to deny that our Arian ancestors
worked the land with plows is not necessarily to reduce them
to barbarity, and readers will be struck on each page of Pictet's
admirable book by the remarkably advanced stage of industrial
development achieved in the earliest phases of the history of
the race."

Some thirty years later, when Saussure offered his "Course in
General Linguistics," he pointed out how misleading it was to
base prehistoric anthropology on the reconstruction of a lost
language. Yet at the same time he reminded his listeners how
attractive the work of the great pioneer had appeared and how
Pictet had "served as a model for many others." [23]

The Hand of Providence

Pictet gave his lyrical pen free rein in the final pages of his
trilogy. The recently discovered Aryas stood out, he said, by
the youthfulness and vigor of their race and the splendor of
their language. Unlike the Hebrews, they treated the soul not
as "the vital breath but as the thinking element" (vol. 3,
p. 531). It was almost exclusively among these peoples that
one finds "the seeds of the spirit of liberty" (p. 528), which
leads to the invention of politics, science, and the arts. The
principle of liberty may well explain why the first Aryas lost
their way in the mists of polytheism before finally conquering
"truth, having experienced error" (p. 536). Once they learned
to represent nature in all its complex reality, however, they
marched with confidence toward Christian monotheism.

If God was the pilot of this world, the "heavenly Father"

(p. 535) relied on a rudder named Providence. The historian's task was to reveal "the role assigned to each race in the drama of the world." To understand God's plan it was enough to follow the providential hand as it moved peoples about on the chessboard of the world. Civilization's two protagonists shared the same stage, but each in its assigned role:

> Faithful guardians of pure monotheism, the Hebrews had a magnificent part in the divine plan, but one wonders where the world would be today if they had remained the sole leaders of mankind. The fact is, while they religiously preserved the principle of truth from which a higher light would one day emanate, Providence had already singled out another race of men to lead the way to further progress.
>
> This was the race of Aryas, blessed from the beginning with the very qualities the Hebrews lacked to become the civilizers of the world. . . . The contrast between the two races is as stark as can be. The Hebrews possess the authority that preserves; the Aryas, the freedom that allows for development. The Hebrews display intolerance, which concentrates and isolates; the Aryas, receptivity, which extends and assimilates; the Hebrews direct their energy toward a single goal; the Aryas engage in incessant activity in all directions. On the one hand is a single compact nationality, on the other a vast race divided into a host of diverse peoples. In both we find exactly what was needed to accomplish the providential designs (vol. 3, pp. 535–536).

As in Renan, everything is ranged under one of two heads. The Hebrews have this, the Aryas have that. The synthesis, Christianity, heralds the radiant future of humanity.

Pictet's maneuver in assigning the monotheistic vocation to the primitive Aryas creates a tension in his work similar to that which we observed in Renan's. And that tension is resolved in a similar way when Pictet deplores the "overly exclusive monotheism" (p. 537) to which conservative Judaism gave rise.

Here again, the passive but essential role of the Hebrews is supposedly to have watched over the slumbering truth of revelation until it could be providentially proclaimed by the Christianized Aryas.[24] Pictet argues that because the first Aryas had a primitive conception of a unique God, a conception that was later "obscured but not completely effaced" (p. 534), the monotheistic idea could one day take root among their descendants, at the time when "most of them" received that idea "in all its purity through the advent of Christianity."

Whereas Renan magnifies the effects of Indo-European polytheism by demonstrating the ambivalence of Semitic values, Pictet attempts to bring out the hidden force in the primordial monotheism of the early Aryas. Different as the two authors are, both praise the taming of the polytheistic spirit, emphasizing the creative freedom that remains once the unbridled imagination is reined in. Similarly, this polytheism could be accommodated within the concept of historical development implicit in the "temperate" monotheism of the Christianized Aryas.[25]

The future of these new Christians was thus assured. "The entire globe" (p. 537) was potentially theirs, "destined as they are to become its rulers." But what has become of the other Aryas, those who represented the element of diversity within the geographic and political unity of the original homeland? Colonized by Europe, these distant oriental brothers were learning to celebrate the "beneficent influence" of modern civilization. The "European Aryas" were on the verge of gratifying their fraternal desires by bringing them "religious illumination and universal progress." Pictet recounted these providential discoveries: "Is it not curious, moreover, to see the Aryas of Europe, after a separation of four to five thousand years, finding their way back, via a vast, circuitous route, to their unknown Indian brothers [so as] to dominate them and bring them the elements of a higher civilization and to discover among them the ancient proof of a common origin?" (vol. 3, p. 537). This colonization is ethical because it is decreed by Providence, and the only privilege the Aryas enjoy is the modest one of being "the principal instrument of God's designs."

The question of how else history could be conceived was also addressed by A.-A. Cournot (1801–1877) in the 1860s.[26] Even if the human races were, like migrating birds, guided by "a marvelous instinct of some kind," human intelligence would insist on introducing the "idea of providence" in order to establish a "moral order" in the realm of freedom (p. 627). In other words, although natural predispositions suffice for animals, lacking as they do any notion of morality, humanity implies precisely the kind of moral character "inherent in the idea of providential direction or coordination." Without such an idea, the human race has no way of grasping the moral dimension of history. It must ascribe order and reason to chance. Thus civilization, which is inseparable from Christianity, must impose its meaning on history: "The overall outline of history: that is the true battlefield for Christian apologetics" (p. 663).

"If man is only an atom in the perceptible world," then there is no way for human beings to comprehend randomness or to perceive morality in history.[27] Society's rules of conduct therefore cannot be based on nature. Max Müller was of the same opinion. Every explanation of the natural world, he believed, must be inscribed in a predetermined order. He made this point in his controversy with Darwin, when he described his terror at the idea of a world deserted by Providence: "Everywhere we see the same desire to explain the universe as we know it without assuming any plan, any purpose, any direction; the same desire to overturn all the barriers, not only those that separate man from animal and animal from plant but also those that separate inorganic from organic matter, the same desire to explain life in terms of chemistry and thought in terms of the motion of nervous molecules."[28]

Pictet expresses his nostalgia for Arian origins through the vision of a fall, a degeneration from primordial monotheism to the dynamic confusion of polytheism. All of this takes place prior to the advent of Christianity. Pictet calls for a new "philosophy of history" that "does not yet exist but is in the process of formation." Bossuet's *Discourse on Universal History* (1681) is no longer adequate for conceptualizing the multiplicity of nineteenth-century man. Where a theology of history had once flourished, Pictet envisions a brand new philosophy that would nevertheless preserve the old Christian conception, according to which human time unfolds against a background of timeless truth. His task is to formulate a modern version of the idea that the historical order has been determined once and for all. Thus the way was paved for manipulators of memory to take over: new generations, faithful to the traditions of the past, would learn to operate the levers of Providence.

✣ Chapter 7

Heavenly Nuptials

Debate continued among theologians. As the similar crystals in a kaleidoscope combine to form an infinite number of images, the ingredients of the Aryan-Semitic controversy turned up everywhere. In the nineteenth century these were ideas around which people could rally as they envisioned colonizing and Christianizing distant lands and peoples who worshiped strange gods.

The writings of Rudolf Friedrich Grau (1835–1893), a German minister and Lutheran apologist, elaborated another possible reaction to the new Indo-European ideas. He transformed the roles of the principal actors, the Aryans (whom he called Indo-Germans[1]) and the Semites, thereby recasting the debate about which of the two was more monotheistic. Grau's aim was to infuse Semitic beliefs into Indo-Germanic cultures. Although these cultures were richly endowed and endlessly adaptable, they suffered a congenital lack of the backbone provided by monotheistic Christianity. Grau's views were in some ways "reactionary," in the sense that they ran counter to the praising of Aryan values that was all too often to the detriment of the Christian church. For Grau, the danger was that Christ would be forgotten: the Cross had to be planted firmly at the center of any venture of cultural understanding. Grau's writings give a surprising new twist to the fortunes of the Aryan-Semitic pair.

After studying theology at Leipzig, Erlangen, and Marburg, Grau was named professor at Königsberg in 1866. His Leipzig colleagues awarded him an honorary doctorate in 1875.[2] Several of his books were translated into English for use by missionaries in converting the Indians.[3] A year after the publication of Renan's *Life of Jesus* in 1863, Grau published a book with a programmatic title: *Semites and Indo-Germans in Their Relation to Religion and Science: An Apology for Christianity from the Standpoint of Folk Psychology.*[4] The aim of the work was to pinpoint, by means of "scientific inquiry" (p. vi), the essential difference between Semites and Indo-Germans. Grau intended to combat paganism by showing the deep opposition between it and Christianity. After acknowledging his debt to Renan, especially in regard to the specific virtues of the Semites and Indo-Germans, Grau voiced his disappointment that the author of the *Life of Jesus* had chosen to treat the Semites as an "inferior race" (p. v, p. 128). How could the Hebrews be treated as inferior stock when they were known to have produced sublime fruit? In the preface Grau contradicts Renan several times but says that he will not bother to add to the many criticisms already leveled at the Frenchman's work.

Grau addresses a series of warnings to the modern world. A glance at the past is all it takes to recognize the fragility of Indo-German glory, whose moment in the sun was brief. Repeated successes did not prevent ultimate failure (p. 260). Now, with the *Kulturkampf,* it was at last possible to call upon the sciences of archaeology and philology to write the history of civilization, and the first urgent task was to plumb the depths of the abyss into which first Athens, then Rome, fell.[5] Grau's appeal was meant as an act of resistance in the face of a danger to which the forgetful Indo-Germans were constantly subject, when they were tempted, as Grau's contemporaries were, by the seductions of secularism. If one did not struggle against dechristianization, against the perils of a new and disillusioned scientific spirit, there was danger of a return to paganism (p. 256). Anyone who tried to divorce Indo-German efficiency from the repository of Semitic meaning controlled by the church threatened the equilibrium of the modern world. The only hope was a proper blend of the monotheistic essence of the Semites with the dynamism of the Indo-Germans within a properly understood Christian context.

Grau was saying nothing new when he suggested that the Hebraic tradition had always guided the course of history. At the same time that Athens flourished thanks to Solon's laws, the Hebrews were deported to Babylon and stripped of their independence. For Grau, this was no coincidence, but a sign of Providence. Was not the flourishing of Christianity contemporaneous with—did it not originate with—the very destruction of this unique people, the only people to set its culture in opposition to Roman power?[6]

The Two Maidens

Grau's views have a logical structure. The peculiarity of some of his pronouncements should not be allowed to obscure the coherence of his overall theological and political argument. His aim is to show that the monotheist torch of the Semites was the only possible link between an omnipotent God and his new chosen people, the Christian faithful. Grau's book ends with a providential marriage that assures the Indo-Germans of a dominant role in history.

Before Grau, Renan had already argued that the Semites had contributed nothing to the world: not science, not philosophy, not art, not politics. "The true religion" (p. 225) was their single, but essential, gift. Their faith had enabled human beings fascinated by the effects of the visible to gain access to an invisible God (p. 217). The Semites were therefore the sole possessors of an atemporal, supernatural, essential truth. Other peoples were indebted for this monotheistic belief to the Hebrews, who had it first. Grau asked himself why this should be so. Why should this people, incapable of philosophy, have laid down the ultimate principle of all true philosophy and then communicated it to the world? The answer is simple (p. 225). The highest truth is not intellectual but ethical; neither intelligible nor imaginative in nature, it lurks hidden in the religious customs that are central to human life. That is where the discrimination between good and evil takes place. Truth was discovered not by the Greeks, a people of philosophers, but by the "unphilosophische Volk der Juden," the unphilosophical Jewish people (p. 227), because truth is not the result of speculation. Truth of this kind can never be a matter of science, nor can it come from the arts that developed in the Indo-Germanic cultures.

The monotheism with which Grau credits the Semites has little to do with the Jews. When he does speak of Jews, it is to recall the wretchedness of a people that has contributed nothing to history other than perhaps its religious potential—and in that case he generally refers to "Hebrews" rather than "Jews." In order to make our way through the maze that Grau lays out before us, we must bear in mind that the Semitic vocation on which he lavishes praise has been invested in the Christian church and is now under its protection.

The Indo-Germans did not receive God's revelation directly. Before they could embrace Semitic monotheism they had to become Christians. They did, however, possess all the qualities necessary for action: an enterprising spirit and the ability to create sciences, arts, and political institutions. Nevertheless, if the temporal Indo-German edifice was to endure, it had to assimilate the Semitic element of eternity in the form of monotheism (pp. 242–243 and 260).[7] Or, to put it another way, the extraordinary dynamism of the Indo-Germans, embodied in the arts and sciences, took on meaning only within the Christian church. Outside it, all temporal works sink into barbarism. To see this, Grau suggests, one has only to contemplate the prodigious creativity of the Indians. Only "the Semitic savor" (p. 251) introduced by Christian domination could save them from unproductive disorder.

The Semites, incapable of progress and unfit for political life, inhabited a kingdom that was not of this world (p. 249). Their timeless religion was notable for its changeless quality, which guaranteed its eternal truth. If the Indo-Germans wish to endure, they must preserve the timeless Semitic portion of their patrimony, which they acquired when they embraced Christ.

While the Semites were notable for the static quality of their values, the Indo-Germans were notable for the constantly changing quality of theirs. With them, everything was always in flux. They were as unstable as their gods, whose images changed with each new political or aesthetic fashion (p. 251). If secular education were to be separated from religious training, divorcing Indo-Germanic from Semitic elements, children would be delivered up to paganism (p. 256).

To protect against the perils of time and the erosion of divine truth by the turbulent currents of Indo-Germanic values, Grau called for a radical ("in den Wurzeln," p. vi) rejection of all forms of paganism. To that end he composed a parable illustrating the providential hand in human history.

Semites, Grau argues, are like women in that they lack the Indo-German capacity for philosophy, art, science, warfare, and politics (pp. 113ff). They nevertheless have a monopoly on one sublime quality: religion, or love of God. This Semitic monism goes hand in hand with a deep commitment to female monogamy. The masculine behavior of the Indo-German, who masters the arts and sciences in order to dominate the natural world, is met with the Semite's feminine response of passivity and receptivity. As the wife is subject to her husband, so the Semites are absolutely permeable to the God who chose them.

The parable begins with God, ardent with desire but clear-headed, faced with a choice between two maidens (pp. 120ff). One, laden with jewels and surrounded by treasures, represents the Indo-German peoples. She dwells in the realm of imagination and devotes her many talents to understanding the things of this world. The other maiden represents the Semites. She is wretchedly dressed and wears no jewelry. The first maiden is a queen, the second a beggar. Yet poor as the beggar is, she possesses one jewel: her love of God, her belief in the Creator. No doubt clouds her mind; she knows that she owes everything to Him. So naturally it is she whom God will choose. Grau then tells us that she is the Virgin Mary. The scene ends with verses from the Song of Songs (1:5–6), proof that appearances can be deceiving: "I am black, but comely, O ye daughters of Jerusalem. . . . Look not upon me, because I am black, because the sun hath looked upon me." The secret of the Semitic treasure is thus transferred from a people chosen by God to the Virgin Mary, elected to be the mother of a human race reborn for all eternity.

The "Feminine Nature" of the Indo-Germans

Thus the monotheistic God wedded his people. But another ordeal lay in store for the Indo-Germans, for whom Grau had quite another wedding in mind (pp. 118ff). Free and virile, conquerors of space and time, the Indo-Germans would nevertheless become subjects of the Semites. Independent in all other areas, they would depend on the Semites for their religion, for they could not become Christians without embracing the Semitic idea of monotheism. The ordeal, Grau explains, was to submit to the religion of a people whose other spiritual faculties were negligible.[8] Until now the Semite has been cast as feminine, embodying pure receptiveness to God. Is Grau now suddenly transforming him into a virile spiritual master, whom the Indo-German must henceforth docilely obey?

Grau's answer is both simpler and more complicated than this characterization would suggest. The Indo-Germans must alter their sexual identity, exchanging extreme virility for total feminine receptiveness, before they can celebrate their marriage with the Semites, here cast in the masculine role of bestowers of meaning. But in order to understand Grau's alchemy, we must first recognize that for him the Semites to whom the Indo-Germans had to submit were the formerly polytheistic peoples who had been liberated from paganism by their new Christian-Semitic outlook (pp. 119ff). In other words, in order to acquire the freedom and independence in religious matters that they enjoyed in all other areas, the Indo-Germans (whether pagans of old or contemporaries of Grau tempted by secularization) first had to catch the monotheistic spark. And they had to continue to keep faith with the Semitic essence, now appropriated by Christianity.

Grau ends his parable with a solemn proclamation of the providential marriage of Indo-German and Semite: "The marriage between Semitic spirit and Indo-Germanic nature is sealed in heaven."[9] Thanks to this wedding, the Indo-Germans receive the true God, embracing the Semitic substance that has flourished in the church of Christ, and can now fulfill their calling *(Beruf)*, which is to rule the world ("die Welt zu beherrschen"; pp. 258, 119)—to rule the world in theory as well as practice, in the arts and through statecraft. Despite this reminder of the imperious virility of the Indo-Germans, Grau concludes his parable by insisting on the interchange of male and female roles in this heavenly marriage. Although God is to the Semite as husband to wife, that does not prevent the Semites from assuming the masculine role vis-à-vis the feminized Indo-Germans. Just as a woman bases her character and the meaning of her life on marriage, so the Indo-Germans discover the meaning of their actions through their conversion to the religion of Christ. The "feminine nature" of the Indo-Germans joins with the "virile spirit" of the Semites (p. 258). Bear in mind that the effeminate Semite, God's obedient monotheistic wife, is a Hebrew, whereas the masculinized Semite who acts as teacher to the Indo-Germans is another Indo-German, a former polytheist saved by conversion to the One True Faith.

This is Grau's leitmotif: although the Greeks and Romans had left nothing but ruins, the Semites will always elude time's clutches. Their vocation, constantly renewed, draws on an inexhaustible treasury, for it comes directly from the eternal God (pp. 260–261). This unalterable patrimony, absorbed by the Christianized Indo-Germans, is modern culture's sole hope of survival. But for this miraculous seizure of the precious mite of monotheism, all the abundant "capital" of the Indo-Germans would lead only to bankruptcy (p. 260). In the end, the meaning of Luther's achievement was to bring about the holy union of Semites and children of Japheth—which, incidentally, was responsible for the success of the Reformation (pp. 235–236).[10]

The Semite's monotheistic enlightenment comes from a place that is essentially and fundamentally remote, but the resplendence emanating from this distance creates proximity. This Semitic spark, unaffected by the ravages of time and sanctified by the church in heavenly matrimony, is essential if the actions of the Indo-Germans in this world of space and time are to have any meaning. Hence Grau, after "semitizing" Christianity, after granting it the unique treasure of the divine, exhorts the Indo-Germans to remain faithful to the church. Fail to heed this injunction, he warns, and risk the loss of your capital and a decline into paganism. The creative gifts of the Indo-Europeans, drawn from temporal sources and tied to the visibility and mutability of their gods, must be subordinated to the unitary order of Christian monotheism, the source of meaning and guarantee of victory.

To bring the true religion of unity to all peoples, to see them kneel "the world over," to abolish the multiplicity of gods, and to ensure that "our civilization" *(Kultur)* becomes a "universal civilization" *(Weltkultur)* conceived in monotheistic Christian terms, Grau wrote a story of humanity that confirmed his wishes and reflected his will to control the future.[11] In so doing the Königsberg theologian contributed yet another chapter to the providential history of mankind.

✿ Chapter 8

Semites as Aryans

South of Budapest, between Lake Balaton and the Danube, lies Szekesfehervar, in ancient times Alba Regia, where Hungarian sovereigns were crowned. There, on June 22, 1850, Ignaz Isaac Jehuda Goldziher was born to a modest family of Jewish leather merchants. Although he received traditional religious instruction, he also attended regular elementary school. Pursuing his classical education along with Talmudic studies, he entered a Cistercian academy at the age of ten. Two years later, the child prodigy published a paper on Jewish prayer.[1] In his diary, which was not published until 1978, Goldziher noted that this brief text had earned him an unsavory reputation among his fellow Jews as a freethinker and "Spinozist."[2]

After his father went bankrupt in 1865, the family was forced to move to Budapest. There the adolescent Goldziher studied for his baccalaureate at the Calvinist gymnasium and attended lectures given at the university by the Orientalist Armin Vambery (1832–1913). At age eighteen Goldziher left for Germany. In Berlin he took courses with the reform rabbi Abraham Geiger (1810–1874) and Moritz Steinschneider (1816–1907), both scholars of "Jewish science" (*Wissenschaft des Judentums*) and experts on the relations between Islam and Judaism in the Middle Ages.[3] Goldziher also met another scholar associated with this group, H. Heymann Steinthal (1823–1899), who encouraged him to learn more about Max Müller's science of myths, folk psychology, and linguistics.[4]

The year 1869 marked a turning point in Goldziher's career.

In Leipzig he became a student of Heinrich Leberecht Fleischer (1801–1888), an eminent philologist who had studied with Silvestre de Sacy (1758–1838), an expert on Arabic, Persian, and Turkish and professor at the Collège de France. Under Fleischer's supervision Goldziher earned his doctorate at the age of twenty, in February 1870.[5] After a brief period of study at Leyden in the Netherlands he returned to Budapest, where he was offered the post of Privatdozent at the university.

He was elected to the Academy of Sciences of Budapest in 1892 and served as correspondent to various learned societies in other countries. Several times he was offered positions in Germany, and in 1894 he was offered a chair at Cambridge, but it was not until 1905 that he obtained the chair of Semitic philology at the University of Budapest. For thirty years prior to that appointment he had earned his living as a paid secretary to the liberal Jewish congregation; since 1900 he had also taught at the rabbinical seminary. But while Goldziher was always interested in Jewish studies, his international reputation rested on his work on Islam.

When he died in Budapest on November 13, 1921, Ignaz Goldziher was a master of Islamic studies.[6] The work of this historian of ideas, philologist, and traveler marked a milestone in the understanding of the Koran and the formation of the Muslim community.[7]

A People's Right to Mythology

In 1876 Goldziher published *Hebrew Myth and Its Historical Development*.[8] Although the book was written in Hungarian, his mother tongue, he took the trouble of translating its four hundred pages into German before submitting it to a publisher. Nonetheless he knew that the work had little chance of reaching the broad audience for which it was written. His aim in this youthful essay was to prove that the Semites had a mythology just as much as other peoples did.

He focused his attention primarily on the Hebrews. Under the influence of the rationalist "Jewish science" of his day, he no doubt hoped to bring critical historical methods to bear on the religion of his ancestors. But he also had another reason for choosing to study Hebrew folklore, because when it came to mythology the Hebrews were reputed to have been even more deprived than other Semitic peoples. Despite an abundance of sources, Hebrew myth had always been the "stepchild" (p. 13) of mythological investigation. As a result, the Hebrews had always been viewed by theologians, Jewish and Christian alike, as confined to a world without images or history. Although this view was demonstrably incorrect, even scholars tended to treat the Hebrews as if untouched by the dangerous but also glorious combination of myth with reason that had been accomplished in Western Europe.[9] The people of Israel were treated as the chosen guardians of monotheism, which other ancient peoples, blinded by polytheism, had supposedly witnessed but forgotten.

In his very first sentence Goldziher warns the reader that he has no intention of "proposing a theory of Hebraic mythology" (p. vii). His aim is to revitalize Semitic studies by introducing models borrowed from the two leading figures in comparative mythology, A. Kuhn (1812–1881) and Max Müller. After naming them as founding fathers of the discipline, Goldziher immediately makes it clear that he will contradict them on certain fundamental points (p. viii). Although he calls himself their disciple—as his book, in its very extravagance, proves—he accepted neither their axioms nor their conclusions.

Goldziher's ambition was thus twofold: to apply the linguistic methods of the new study of mythology, which had already proved so valuable in Aryan studies, to Semitic material; and to demonstrate that the method was scientifically valid by proving its universal applicability.[10] For Goldziher, the second aim was crucial, for he hoped to prove that at some point in their history all peoples, without exception, invented myths in response to psychological necessity.

Goldziher accordingly sought to pinpoint the source of all myths that had originated in the Semitic deserts. Paying close attention to atmospheric changes, to the darkness of the night sky and the brightness of daylight, he searched, like Kuhn, for the theme of storms and, like Max Müller, for the great solar myth.[11] These techniques had provided a successful approach to Indo-Germanic mythology.[12] In the poetry of the Bible Goldziher accordingly found traces of a solar Yahweh who used his arrows (rays) to combat a serpent either fleeing (like lightning) or coiling itself against the rain. Conflict between a star and a monster (also found in the story of Jonah) occurred in many other mythologies. Here, however, the insistence on monotheism, a part of the history of the people of Israel, necessitated the substitution of Yahweh for the sun (pp. 33, 329). Elsewhere, following Steinthal, he argues that not even his "most skeptical" reader can deny that Samson's struggles represent the battle of light against darkness. He observes, for example, that Samson's Hebrew name, *Shimshon,* immediately suggests *shemesh,* "the sun" (pp. 25–26 and 300). Apart from these mechanical applications of theories in vogue at the time, Goldziher offers, if not a theory of Hebrew mythology, at least an overview of the slow historical and political process whereby the Hebrews moved from a polytheistic stage, comparable to the Aryans', to a form of monotheism that was by no means original.

Goldziher had set himself a difficult task. The idea of a Hebrew mythology seemed strange, all the more so as students were never taught to read the Bible as a series of archaic legends, whereas classical training prepared them to recognize the mythical in Greek and Roman narratives. Traditional Arabic legends seemed equally remote (pp. xxvii and 209ff). Yet stories of alliances and disputes between the stars could also be found in "true nomadic myths" (p. xxix).

Goldziher was thus in a position to appreciate the resistance to the notion that all peoples, including Semites, have myths. This resistance, which he hoped to overcome, did not stem solely from theology. Strangely enough, old religious arguments for the supposed mythological incapacity of certain cultures had acquired new scientific legitimacy through the idea of "race." Race was at the root of the scholarly claim that not all peoples are capable of mythology. Applying comparative methods to study of the Semitic region of the world required overcoming the "prejudice" (*Vorurtheil,* p. xv) that there exist "unmythological races" (*unmythologische Rassen*).

Without rejecting the axioms of the comparative mythology of his day, Goldziher made the following argument: Myth describes how individuals in a community perceive natural phenomena. If a group of individuals becomes a people only when it shares a worldview reflected in its myths, then a people without mythology is inconceivable.[13] Mythological culture therefore plays an indispensable role in the formation and development of any society. No people can escape the limitations of the human mind, which uses language to invent myths in order to formulate perceptions (or apperceptions) of the natural environment. To say that a race is incapable of inventing myth is, from the standpoint of folk psychology, to posit the existence of a "pathological race" (p. xv). If works of ethnology allude to peoples among whom "no trace of myth" can be found, their error, according to Goldziher, is to count only complex fables as mythology while excluding simpler narratives.

Goldziher and other students of comparative mythology believed that myths used figurative language to represent the impressions made on the senses by natural phenomena. Two factors therefore influenced the development of mythology. One was psychology: the laws governing the "life of the soul" (*das Leben der Seele,* p. 45) were universal, independent of a people's ethnological situation or racial characteristics. The other was cultural history: myths always reflected the history of a particular people. The mythology of any community was therefore closely intertwined with its social, economic, and political history. Since all peoples are psychologically capable of producing mythology, the diversity of myth reflects the diversity of social life. Hunters and fishermen perceive nature differently when they become nomads or farmers. Their fears, desires, and interests are transformed; their myths undergo metamorphosis. Myths are thus influenced by historical events; when Goldziher points out that myth cycles are slow to change, it is to emphasize the importance of attending to periods of long duration. Comparative mythology must seek to understand myth in terms of "broad cultural periods" (p. 62) rather than "small chronological sections." This culture-historical view of myth also leads to the hypothesis that "myth is an accurate mirror of the cultural stage" (p. 46) in which it originates. [14]

Goldziher used the word "race" in its everyday sense rather than as a causal determinant of group behavior. His analysis borrowed heavily from the "psychology of peoples" (*Völkerpsychologie*) developed by M. Lazarus (1824–1903). Lazarus regarded this discipline as a "psychology of humankind" (*Menscheitspsychologie,* p. 46), whose aim was to identify the general laws of the human mind beyond the apparently diverse behavior of different groups. Goldziher took care to distinguish *Völkerpsychologie* from *Rassenpsychologie*. The purpose of the "psychology of peoples" was to demonstrate that the same laws govern the "life of the soul" everywhere and thus determine the behavior of all peoples. As alien and remote as two peoples may be, their psychological drives are the same. "There is no such thing as the psychology of a particular race." [15]

Hence the science of mythology must not subordinate itself to racial classification (p. 21). Indeed, proper use of comparative mythology shows that the same fundamental patterns underlie the myths of "all mankind, without distinction as to race" (p. 108). These mythological types, as universal as the perception of sunlight and darkness, are not "specifically Aryan." Without denying the diversity of historical cultures, Goldziher nevertheless wants to treat "Hebrew myth using categories common to all humanity."

Max Müller may have been right, Goldziher argued, when he criticized Renan's notion of a "monotheistic instinct" (pp. 10 and 316), but he was wrong to think that "mythological phraseology" was peculiar to the Aryan race.[16] He was also wrong to claim that the Semitic vocabulary made it impossible to "forget the attributive meaning" of words (p. 49), as if the transparency of Semitic words permitted clear identification of each distinct natural phenomenon, whereas the Aryan tongues blurred meaning and thus magically gave rise to mythology. Goldziher therefore contradicted Max Müller's idea that obliviousness to the original meaning of Aryan words was the root and "unhealthy" source of myth. He denied that confusing the meaning of words for natural phenomena was necessary for myth to arise. Naming the perception of a natural phenomenon was enough to create a myth (p. 50). The Sun, the Moon, the Dawn—these prototypes of ancient mythology were not the result of any forgetfulness or confusion. Helios (according to the Greeks, the brother of Selene and Eos) and the Latin Aurora did not arise from any mysterious phenomenon of language (p. 50).

Goldziher's goal was to de-aryanize mythologizing by demonstrating that it was a universal human activity. He wished to do so by importing into the Semitic world methods successfully applied in Aryan studies. As promised, he reveals to his readers the solar and lunar aspects of various figures in Hebrew literature and, where possible, in their Arabic counterparts. Thus Adam and Eve (p. 255), Noah (p. 383), and the patriarchs (pp. 21ff, 38, and 109ff) become representatives of a solar mythology, either because of their actions or because their names recall the sun (Adam, for example, evokes the sun's red rays).[17] *Elohim,* a plural name for a singular God, can be construed either as singular or as a majestic plural because it serves as a reliquary of Semitic polytheism (p. 327).

Although Goldziher argues that Hebrew mythology can and should be studied in the same way as Greek and Indian myth cycles, he nevertheless finds that, even when supplemented with the rabbinical commentaries in the Haggadah (pp. 34ff), the biblical material is less rich than the great frescoes of the Aryans (p. 21). The "original core" (p. 23) of Hebrew myth no doubt arose, as did the myths of other peoples, out of natural phenomena. The acts and words of the patriarchs, and even their very names, are marked by an interpretation of natural phenomena. Nevertheless, consideration of the "historical development"[18] of these myths makes one thing clear: what distinguishes the Hebrews is the fact that they transformed their mythological material into historical figures, into ancestral founders of a theological and political system. Whereas the polytheism of the Greeks allowed them to flesh out their heroes and deities, the monotheism of the Hebrews forced them to repress their mythology and turn it into history (pp. 23–24).

The national history of the Hebrews began in Canaan when nomadic tribes crossed the right bank of the Jordan to claim a homeland (pp. 281ff). The level of their religious and political culture was so inferior to that of the natives that the Hebrews borrowed kingship and other institutions from them as well as from their new neighbors, the Phoenicians. For Goldziher no other historical explanation is plausible. A nomadic people "without a political past" (p. 293) could not possibly have created an urban culture overnight. The temple, the priesthood, and the magistracy were based on their Phoenician counterparts (pp. 292ff).

Thus the conquerors, an intellectually and spiritually impoverished people (*das geistig arme Volk,* p. 299) discovered the cultural riches of the Canaanites and Phoenicians. The vestiges of their nomadic mythology were transformed by political pressures at the time of the "awakening of national consciousness" (p. 303). In the past "as in modern times," national passions helped to shape myths. National heroes were given a prehistoric genealogy to bolster their legitimacy. While Abraham was the father of all peoples, he was also the ancestor of the Hebrews (Genesis 14:13, 17:4–5), so his descendants may feel justified in blaming their enemies (p. 306). Ham, who felt no shame when he found his father Noah sleeping naked, was the father of the Canaanites, who bore Noah's curse (Genesis 9:18–26). "National passions" (p. 307) thus transformed Noah, the ancient hero of nomadic solar myth, into an ancestral figure whose curse explained and if need be justified the Hebrews' conquest of Canaan.[19]

Goldziher devotes an entire chapter to the close ties between the ancient myths and the new national identity of the Hebrews. As conquerors in enemy territory, they needed historical legitimation (*ein historischer Rechtstitel,* p. 303). As they reformulated the ancient Hebrew mythology, they conjured up the image of the prehistoric ancestors who first settled in the land of Canaan. Mythical figures were nationalized into historical actors by the new community consciousness. Goldziher explains the "political idea" (p. 331) behind this move: to argue after the fact that the need for a national territory went all the way back to the "time of the patriarchs," so that when the conquest was complete the Hebrew nation could claim the conquered land as having been its "property" forever.

With the emergence of a national consciousness, the Hebrews would gradually free themselves from the land of Canaan. But they would never eliminate the foreign influences that constituted "the best part" (p. 315) of the Hebraic spirit. The national awakening had enabled them to "assimilate" *(verarbeiten)* foreign values and to integrate them into an independent worldview.

Goldziher returns to this idea, to which he seems particularly attached, in the final pages of his book: "Originality is not the only criterion of the miraculous" (p. 390). A civilization that develops by assimilating foreign elements can still constitute "a harmonious whole."

Rather than extol beginnings or yearn for a golden age, Goldziher preferred to see the values of a developing culture in temporal perspective. A nation could distinguish itself by its ability to "digest" alien cultural forms and yet still demonstrate independent creative powers. In this connection, Goldziher raised a question that many contemporary specialists found troubling. Did ancient Iran influence Hebrew literature or vice versa? Did the Aryans teach the Semites all they knew, or were the Semites the parents of civilization? Goldziher's answer is that it is just as misleading to look for an Iranian source for every verse in the Pentateuch as it is wrong to deny that there was any such influence (p. 389). "We do not save the honor of Hebraic [literature] by insisting that the Iranians were pupils in Hebrew schools" (p. 391).

Yahweh's "Cosmopolitan Character"

The high point in the history of Hebraic religion involved an "ingenious creation" (p. 348): "the Yahweh-thought" *(der Jahve-Gedanke)*. Even if this had been the Hebrews' "only original thought," it would have assured them "a lasting place" in world history.

The precise origin of the "Yahweh-thought" cannot be ascribed, nor can the moment of its appearance be specified. Goldziher therefore chooses to focus on its discernable historical effects in the texts of the prophets. Its only possible rival in the history of religion is "the Allah-thought" *(der Allâh-Gedanke)*, which according to Goldziher does not attain the same "religious height" (p. 349). Yahweh was known to the pre-Islamic Arabs, and the name Allah existed in pre-Islamic theology. Although the two divine notions share many common attributes, history divided Yahweh from Allah. The prophesies of the Hebrew and Arab prophets forged a unique destiny for each (p. 350).

Goldziher showed no interest in the origins of Yahweh. He cared only about tracing Yahweh's influence after the prophets, who were neither men of culture nor scholars, made him a factor in the religious history of the Hebrews. Impassioned enthusiasts but poor politicians, the prophets were above all extraordinary "representatives of national individuality and independence" (p. 356). Since Yahweh was—to a certain extent at least—a national god, the prophets chose him to be "the unique God." [20]

But Yahweh's message was no more consistently or exclusively national than that of the prophets. Though "first recognized by the Hebrew people" (pp. 361–362), Yahweh eventually commanded the recognition of "all humanity" thanks to the prophetic conception of the one God. He answered the prophets' call for a "world history." Goldziher detects this "cosmopolitan character" of Yahweh in the prophetic writings of various periods. He also detects a perpetual movement back and forth between the particular and the universal in texts where Yahweh loves all peoples yet grants one "the lion's share" (p. 362; Isaiah 2:2–4, 19:24–25; Zephanaiah 3:9–10).

The exile and diaspora of the Hebrews coincided with the most impassioned moments of prophetism. Far from the Temple of Jerusalem a religion of compromise developed, torn between the prophets and the priests (pp. 367–368). Later, however, all myths were subsumed in Yahweh. "In the popular mind" (p. 372), God was now capable of calming the storm or bringing light to overwhelming darkness. Thus when the monotheist in Job asks where rain, dew, ice, and frost come from, the whole system of nature points to a single cause: Yahweh (Job 38:28–29). "Myth, at this stage, was entirely defeated" (p. 372).

Goldziher substantiates his case over many chapters. To those who are willing to accept the existence of Semitic mythology but not of Hebraic legend, he attempts to prove that the major figures of the Old Testament could have originated in myths and that they were not borrowed from any outside source (p. 15). He then tries to demonstrate the "historical development" of Hebrew mythology over a very long period of time. Once Hebrew myths took on a political and national purpose, they began to decline under the combined effects of the Yahweh-thought and prophetic teaching. Semitic monotheism then reached the height of its development.

In Goldziher's writing there is no trace of a dominant "instinct" (Renan) or of an original monotheism (Max Müller). While mythology and the religion that grows out of it (pp. 16–17) reflect a universal need, their collective representations are shaped by the social and political history of each nation. Stunned that some authors congratulated the Hebrews for a Bible pure of all mythology, Goldziher exclaims: "As if myth were an abomination, a taint on the human heart" (p. 15). To those searching for an image-free golden age, he says that mythology does not stem from "a sin of the spirit owing to free will." Hence it is unlikely that scholars will ever discover "the chosen people capable of dispensing with myth."

The views that Goldziher opposes all stem from theories based on the idea of primitive monotheism. This idea, accepted not only by ecclesiastics but also by scholars "less influenced by theological assumptions" (p. 316), grew out of the ancient intuition that out of one came many. Goldziher deplores the fact that "old Hume" (p. 317) was not heard on this point. In the *Natural History of Religion* (1757) he wrote:

It seems certain that, according to the natural progress of human thought, the ignorant multitude must first entertain some groveling and familiar notion of superior powers before they stretch their conception to that perfect Being who bestowed order on the whole frame of nature. We may as reasonably imagine that men inhabited palaces before huts and cottages or studied geometry before agriculture as assert that the Deity appeared to them a pure spirit, omniscient, omnipotent, and omnipresent, before he was apprehended to be a powerful though limited being with human passions and appetites, limbs, and organs. The mind rises gradually, from inferior to superior: by abstracting from what is imperfect, it forms an idea of perfection.[21]

Like matter in the universe, the human spirit, Goldziher believed, is in constant flux. Polytheism, he argued, is a highly developed form of mythology whose ultimate end lies in the monotheism toward which all religious thought evolves. The human vision of nature and conception of politics also tends toward greater unity and abstraction. Albert Réville (1826–1906) exemplifies a similar line of thought, though he is quicker than Goldziher to recognize "suspicions, seeds, [and] anticipations of monotheism" in the older polytheisms: "Finally, it is clear that the human spirit, as it observes and reflects in obedience to that imperious law hidden in the depths of its being, the logical quest for unity, raises itself ever nearer to monotheism. But this movement, impeded by the prestige of traditions and habits, is very slow, and we must be careful not to place at the beginning what could only have come about at the very end."[22]

Goldziher shared this conviction. Religious thought has a

history, in which monotheism figures as "a historical moment in the evolution" of polytheism (p. 318). Goldziher answers those who would cloister the Hebrews within primitive monotheism by bringing to bear contemporary concepts borrowed from the arsenal of comparative mythology and philology. Since everything, in his view, can be explained by cultural evolution and nothing by origins, no people can be excluded from the social history of mankind. There is no such thing as a people living in a state of nature (*sogenannte Naturvölker,* p. 323) and there is no sanctified people, for the same reason that there was no sudden revelation of religion to Moses. Monotheism slowly developed out of polytheism under the influence of historical factors that must now be accounted for by the new sciences of religion.

Where other scholars believed they saw a common Semitic origin for myths of Eden (pp. 386ff) or the Flood (pp. 381ff), Goldziher saw historical borrowings. Why appeal to the magic of a "nebulous" (p. 380) prehistory when we can now study the Assyrian-Babylonian writings on which the Hebrews drew during their exile? In opposition to the "ill-conceived piety" (p. 390) that attributes so much to Hebrew antiquities, the author of *The Mythology of the Hebrews* reiterated his credo: there is nothing dishonorable about borrowing cultural elements and transforming them into an invention of one's own. Instead of a drama of origins, in which each nation attempts to envelop its ancestors in an aura of immemorial autochthony, Goldziher proposed that proper credit be given to cultural borrowing and exchange. In that way each people could preserve its identity while at the same time recognizing the multiplicity of its historical, religious, and political origins.

In the course of his diatribes against the alleged splendor of primitive times Goldziher also demolished the notion of a providential birthplace of both the Aryan and Semitic peoples (p. 390, n. 1).[23] If the two groups shared certain legends, it was not because they had a common homeland but because peoples from each group had encountered and engaged in exchange with peoples from the other. It was the historian's task to identify the traces sometimes left by these encounters.

At the end of his book Goldziher expressed his high hopes for the discoveries he believed would flow from the study of Assyrian-Babylonian myths made possible by the decipherment of cuneiform tablets. He mentioned the titles of two publications by the Assyriologist George Smith (1840–1876) that appeared in 1876, the same year as Goldziher's book.[24] Smith demonstrated the existence of similar themes in Chaldean and biblical creation myths and noted "concordances and differences" (p. 398) between Babylonian and biblical versions of the Flood.

Renan's Dogmatic Elegance

The chief aim of *The Mythology of the Hebrews* (1876) was to demolish Renan's contention (cited in French by Goldziher on the fourth page of his book) that "the Semites never had a mythology" (vol. 8, p. 148). Almost twenty years later, on November 27, 1893, Goldziher was invited by the Academy of Sciences in Budapest to deliver a memorial address in honor of the eminent foreign member who had died the year before: Renan. The occasion offered Goldziher the opportunity to reread the *History of the People of Israel* and to write a hundred pages on "Renan as orientalist."[25]

After hailing Renan's monumental oeuvre, Goldziher reaffirms his criticism of France's eminent Hebraist: to the end of his life, Goldziher argues, Renan was blinded by his desire to "attribute to the entire Semitic race phenomena that occurred only among the Hebrew people, and then only in the historical period" (Memorial, p. 29).

Fascinated by the era of the prophets and by Islam's religious revelations, Renan worked variations on the theme of the "monotheistic instinct" without taking historical events into account. Ultimately he ascribed to the entire Semitic race a primitive monolatry for which Goldziher contends there is absolutely no evidence.

Renan also imagined a strict division of roles between Aryans and Semites, an unbreachable border between the land of many gods and that tyrannized by the "monotheistic instinct." To a historian who was as much of a positivist as Goldziher, nothing could be more implausible: "It was solely in surrender to armed violence, and in appearance only, not with a sincere heart, that the Arabs bowed down before Allah, the one God their prophet had borrowed from abroad. When they finally became monotheists, their national life was not transformed in any way other than that experienced by Aryan populations when they became Christian" (Memorial, p. 29).

Here we recognize Goldziher's constant concern with treating Aryans and Semites within the context of a single critical history of mythology. He felt that Renan failed to live up to the strict standards of positivist history and that in the absence of sources he allowed himself to make free use of analogies (Memorial, p. 63). His whole "comparative history of religion" was actually based on nothing more than analogy coupled with "racial psychology," and some of the analogies involved were no more than topographical, as when the vast emptiness of the desert was adduced as the source of monotheism (Memorial, p. 78). Renan may have been a "great skeptic," but his work bears the stamp of unremitting "dogmatism." [26] Despite occasional recantings, his work remained "until the end of his life" based on the concept of the "monotheistic instinct" (Memorial, p. 30). Renan's central hypothesis was thus unacceptable to Goldziher or to anyone else versed in the subtleties of Hebrew mythology.

As early as 1876 Goldziher was already pointing out that

the French scholar's work grew out of an "elegance of representation characteristic of everything Renan writes" and ultimately hardened into "dogma" (p. 4).[27] At the Academy in Budapest Goldziher repeated this charge, demonstrating the extent to which *a priori* assumptions and "philosophical premises" (Memorial, p. 30) informed Renan's work. Moreover, his linguistic conception of national psychology forced him to resort to a form of anthropology in which religious phenomena were shorn of their historical dimension. Hence he was forced to ascribe religious facts to a cause beyond or parallel to history, such as a natural characteristic or instinct: "The spiritual evolution of peoples is not rooted in instincts prior to their historical life but results from contacts established in the course of historical existence" (Memorial, p. 30).

The Dream of a Messianic Science

Where Renan liked to give simple, unambiguous answers to complex questions, Goldziher preferred a multiplicity of explanatory factors.[28] For him, there could be no single, isolated, elementary source of religion. Psychological factors doubtless played a part in the development of religious feeling, but that part varied from place to place. The Hungarian scholar insisted that religious phenomena be examined in light of their historical context and understood in relation to the social representations from which they sprang. *The Dogma and Law of Islam,* published in Heidelberg in 1910, began with detailed consideration of the state of religious studies and with a suggestion that the whole question of the origins of religion be reexamined:

> It is now man's innate consciousness of causality, now his feeling of dependence, now his "intuition of the infinite," now his renunciation of the world that is said to be the dominant emotion that produces the seed of religion.

I believe that this phenomenon of the psychic life of mankind is far too complex to ascribe to a *single* cause. Nowhere does religion appear to us as an abstraction independent of specific historical conditions. It manifests itself, in higher or lower forms, through concrete phenomena, which vary with social conditions. Among the various phenomena that reflect the power of religion, one of the wellsprings of the religious impulse mentioned above, or perhaps even another not mentioned, may well play a *preponderant* role, but that does not exclude the possible involvement of other factors.[29]

Goldziher aligned the course of religious history with his view of the development of human thought. Once freed from its mythical matrix, religion steadily "raised itself" (he refers to "higher or lower forms") toward monotheism, which, in its final phase, inaugurated the history of scientific understanding. He firmly warns against "any confusion between the original myth and religion or even the consciousness of God" (p. 16). In order to understand the progress of religion, Goldziher uses comparative mythology to retrace the various stages of its development. In ancient times myth became associated with language as the human spirit sought to capture in words "the rain and the sun's rays." At this stage it was "psychologically" impossible to practice religion in any other way. In the age of mythology the "consciousness of God" (*Gottesbewusstsein*, p. 17) was still beyond reach. Later, when myths had evolved to the point where they were increasingly "incomprehensible" and "senseless," their destination changed. Some mythical material subsequently evolved along the path of "history or religion," while the rest continued on its old course. Those mythological elements not assimilated by religion or history entered into the myths and legends that all peoples share.

The "conscious existence" (*die bewusste Existenz*, p. 63) of myths thus comes to an end when the primitive forms metamorphose into gods: "Theology dethrones myth." But what is effaced is only a particularly vibrant form of the myth; not until the monotheistic process reaches its ultimate stage of Yahvism does religion become "negation" (*Verneinung,* p. 64) of the mythic element. Once mythology has been dispelled, the field is clear for religion to take its place. Then, in the final emancipation, religion becomes identified with "scientific consciousness" (*wissenschaftliche Bewusstsein,* p. 17).

Goldziher had absolutely no doubt on this score. "It is our sacred conviction," he wrote in *The Mythology of the Hebrews* (p. xxiii), that the science of religious phenomena is of the highest importance for "the religious life of the present time." Isolating myth brings religion to the fore. And whatever reveals the ideal monotheism, purged of all remnants of paganism, takes us to "the original living source of all truth and all morality."

In other words, religious ideas must henceforth be based on the results of the science of religion.[30] Goldziher, a Jew, thus invited Muslim readers to draw the vital core of their beliefs from his works on Islam. Far from imperiling his monotheistic faith, his critical spirit seems to have heightened his respect for the moral values of Judaism and Islam.

In a lecture delivered to a Jewish audience in Stockholm in 1913, Goldziher praised the faith of his ancestors as a "sacred tradition of the idea of God, which began with obsolete fetishistic forms and developed into the purely spiritual and moral idea of God." For Goldziher, this ancestral tradition, whose supreme value lay in "making life more idealistic, more moral, and more agreeable," also justified tolerance of other traditions: "Every form of religion is a product of traditions. Each is a 'path of salvation.' This idea incorporates the notion of tolerance. Tolerance is logically implicit in it, not extracted as a concession."[31]

The desire to combine a critical history of religious thought with an advanced form of monotheistic religion reflected Gold-

ziher's idea of liberal Judaism with its recent enthusiastic embrace of emancipation. This was a Judaism that dreamed of
freedom from all religious dogmatism, political totalitarian-
ism, and nationalist pride, and based its hope for survival on
the universal values of science. Thus liberated from the ghetto,
Judaism could attempt to forge new social and cultural alliances by identifying not only with traditional Jewish practice
and law but also with Jewish history and memory. It was to be
a return to original sources, but with the old messianism replaced by a new universal faith based on science.

As a young scholar, Goldziher had proposed a scrupulous use
of comparative mythology for the purpose of integrating ancient Hebrew legends with the folklore of other peoples. In
asking the Christian West to recognize the "mythology of the
Hebrews," he was asking his contemporaries to assimilate the
Jews into European culture. By the end of his life Goldziher
had suffered both as a Jew and as an Islamic specialist. He
witnessed the rise of anti-Semitism in his homeland and the
heightening of tensions between Jews and Arabs in Palestine.
In the spring of 1919, Bela Kun, a Hungarian Bolshevik of
Jewish descent, formed a revolutionary government that was
subsequently overthrown by Admiral Horthy and the forces of
"savage anti-Semitism" that supported him.[32] It was in this
context that the geologist Lajos Loczy, a member of the Academy of Sciences, made insulting remarks about the Jew Goldziher. After publicly responding to these insults, Goldziher re-
signed from the Academy.[33]

Despite this incident, Goldziher did not become a Zionist.
The following year his childhood friend Max Nordau (1849–
1923) wrote asking him to come to Jerusalem, where, he said,
a university was "on the verge of being established."[34] The celebrated scholar refused, reminding Nordau that he had refused
similar invitations from other universities. Leaving Hungary
seemed to him "a sacrifice from the standpoint of the father-

land." This time, however, he no doubt had another reason for declining. In his letter Nordau had alluded to the "friendly relations" that Goldziher "could establish between Jews and Arab Muslims." Surely Goldziher would have been in a better position than any other Jew to have carried out such a mission of peace. Nevertheless, he chose to turn down his childhood friend, now a philosopher and physician as well as cofounder of the World Zionist Organization.[35] But in the same year, 1920, he made this public statement to one of his disciples, a young Christian Arab from Mossoul: "I have lived for your nation and for my own. If you return to your homeland, tell this to your brothers."[36]

Chapter 9

Secrets of the Forge

The Bible continued to haunt the new Indo-European archives throughout the nineteenth century. The comparison of the Indo-European with the Semitic language system revived old controversies about the supposed polytheism of the former and monotheism of the latter. While the techniques of philological scholarship evolved and comparativism prospered everywhere, old theological questions continued to make their influence felt.

In the works of Renan, Pictet, Max Müller, and Grau, Christ remained a central figure in the conceptualization of Indo-European civilization. The new religious sciences attempted to treat all religions in the same way and yet to impose a Christian providential meaning on the new comparative order. The very organization of religious data was affected by older hierarchical classifications. The cataloging of peoples and faiths reflected the belief that history was moving in a Christian direction.

Although different schools of thought produced variations on the providential theme, there were subtle links between fervently Christian discourse and supposedly secular work in the new disciplines of theology and religious science.[1] Theoretical adversaries shared a similar romantic sensibility. They also approached the origins of Christian monotheism with the same set of genealogical questions. Aryans who embraced the One God looked to the Hebrews to teach them how monotheism could be universal yet exclusive. In this they reflected the desires of a society whose dream was to regenerate itself by discovering, whole and intact, its own sources.[2] The nineteenth-century authors we have looked at all claimed the mantle of some remote ancestor while working to free themselves from the past that ancestor represented. Thus the Aryans were likened to adolescents and contrasted with the Semites, said to remain in an arrested state of childhood: everything must evolve toward realization of its implicit potential. The old was rejected in favor of the new, yet the new remained attentive to the past as harbinger of what was still to come. Dreams of purity abounded in an age that aspired to a revaluation of all values.

The French Revolution was still fresh in everyone's mind. The question of the extent to which the Revolution was or was not a product of Christianity was a topical one. When François Furet says that for Edgar Quinet Christianity was "betrayed by the Roman Catholic Church and periodically rediscovered by heretics faithful to the words of Jesus," a view that obviously owed much to the Reformation, we are reminded of Renan.[3] Behind the anticlerical demeanor of the former student of Saint-Sulpice we recognize a "dechristianizer" of the sort whose opposition to Catholic tradition is all the more fierce because he hopes for a return to the religion of Jesus.[4]

An old Hebrew text provided one of Western Christendom's founding myths. God, his face shrouded in eternity, created the world in six days simply by breathing the syllables of certain words in a language that dispelled chaos. And so there was light, the light of day, and the darkness of night, and the water, and the heavens, and the earth covered with grasses and fruits, and the stars, and animals of every kind, and finally man and woman. In the Garden of Eden man in turn used language to name every one of God's creatures (Genesis 2:19–20). The story of Genesis is thus the story of language in action—first the language of God, then the language of man. This creative power of the word was revived by the Gospel of John.

Although the role of linguistics in the development of the

human sciences in the nineteenth century is clear, we must be careful not to minimize the importance of these biblical references, shared by scholars and theologians alike. The Bible remained important even though scientists consciously sought to free themselves from its community of meaning. The desire to do science by grouping languages into families and subjecting them to such rigorous new notions as comparison and transformation paved the way for the human sciences without nullifying old options. The new forms of knowledge paid heavy tribute to the past, of which scientists were, often unbeknownst to themselves, the heirs. In order to envision its future, the West still had no choice but to comprehend itself in terms of kinship and filiation with all their attendant complexity.

In K'ai-Feng the Jesuits had hoped to discover a different kind of temporality, an unbroken thread that could be traced all the way back to the time of Moses (see Chapter 2). This intact strand would, they thought, provide a reliable vantage point outside time. Hebrew, the sacred language, would provide objective proof of providential revelation, annunciation of the Word of Christ.

Later, many scholars who discovered the Indo-European world hoped to lay their hands on archives that would document the history of humankind back to the beginning, to the first Aryans, the pastors of civilization. They hoped to find, in an Indian temporality that paralleled the Christian, primitive documents in the supreme tongue, Aryan, which would tell of the origins of a long-forgotten continent. At the turn of the century Sylvain Lévi took note of these biblical certitudes and their effects:

> Despite the advanced state of civilization evident in the earliest Aryan tongues, [and] despite other scientific evidence, old biblical prejudices and presumptuous enthusiasm caused people to believe that they had discovered the birth of language if not the creation of man. . . . They therefore declared that primitive

Aryan was monosyllabic and consisted exclusively of roots. Monsieur de Saussure's theory of disyllabic roots, useful as it is for explaining previously obscure forms, has today foundered on this unshakable prejudice.[5]

This rediscovered Aryan territory became the primitive homeland of Western man in search of legitimation. One of the many functions of Indo-European research was to provide answers to a series of questions that first became urgent in the nineteenth century, questions pertaining to the origins and vocation of a Western world in search of a national, political, and religious identity.

In contrast to the Aryans, the Hebrews possessed the secret of making their way outside of time. The Semites, together with their language, cannot be assigned to a moment in history. Having no connection to the vectors of time, they have no place in the evolution of history.

Goldziher, by encouraging his contemporaries to treat Semitic narratives as myths and incorporate them into the growing corpus of comparative philology, was really asking that the Hebrew Bible be assimilated into the cultural patrimony of Western scholarship. A Hungarian Jew and Islamicist thus turned to myth in the hope of persuading his Christian contemporaries that the Hebrews were not mere passive witnesses of the providential message they had revealed, and were not to be identified with an invariable truth so as to exclude them from historical change. Instead, he argued, they had as much claim as the Aryans to being the founders of the great civilization that will join all societies in the unified history of humanity.

But Christian theology sought to mark its progress by invoking the testimony of an immobilized witness, a witness that had not changed since Christ burst the spatial and temporal boundaries within which monotheism had once been confined. The one Truth then combined with the plurality of the real to take on a variety of historical forms. As a guarantor of the essence of Christianity (tempered by certain Aryan values), Semitic monotheism was called upon to rehearse the prehistory of humankind: the truth *before* the beginning of the *present era,* whose inception was the work of Aryans, adepts of the gods and of natural phenomena and experts in mediation. Once liberated from the mists of polytheism, the Aryans turned their talent for multiplicity loose on the stage of history, incorporating the recently adopted Christian revelation.

These were some of the stories that the nineteenth century, an age in search of fundamental truth, told about its past. Meanwhile, in opera houses throughout Europe—a Europe tormented by revolutionary fervor that often ended in disillusionment—ancient gods began to sing. With Jakob Grimm's *Germanic Mythology* (1835) and Schopenhauer's writings at his side, Richard Wagner (1813–1883) produced a four-part Aryan epic.[6] The *Ring of the Nibelung* was composed over a period of more than twenty-five years (from 1848 to 1874) and based on a poem written between 1848 and 1853. Imbued with a Christianity from which he had just escaped, Wagner dreamed of Germanizing the Greek miracle: he hoped to give Germany a new divine theater by transposing the ancestral myths revealed by romantic science onto the operatic stage.[7]

In a world populated with celestial figures (Wotan and his cohort) and underground creatures (the Nibelungen) we meet a lonely hero, the handsome Siegfried. As a child he is raised by a monstrous dwarf, Mime the blacksmith. Though the "filthy midget" has all the attributes of a master, he has none of the talent.[8] The knowledge he possesses is useless, and he is incapable of teaching Siegfried anything. When Siegfried orders him to forge the broken pieces of Wotan's sword, he cannot do it. In the end it is the disciple, Siegfried, who forges Notung, the sword of salvation. The roles are thereby reversed: the disciple becomes the master and first enslaves, then kills, his crippled stepfather. Neither man can understand the other. Siegfried's one obsession is to discover the name of his father and mother, but when he tries to extort this information from Mime, the dwarf claims to have been both. Despite Siegfried's insistence—"it is from you that I must learn who my father and mother are" (I.24)—Mime will not reveal the secret. He dies on Siegfried's sword without having divulged that the hero is the product of divine incest.[9]

A master who cannot teach and a disciple who ends up killing his master: what Satgé calls the "circuits of knowledge" had indeed broken down.[10] Theodor W. Adorno (1903–1969) suggests that Mime and his brother, the monster Alberich, were stand-ins for the Jew, the object of Wagner's anti-Semitic obsessions.[11] Here, far from academia, a question of filiation took the form of a dramatic allegory. While scholars pursued their genealogical theories in a realm somewhere between science and theology, Wagner, through his choice of learned sources and lyrical devices, dramatized an important aspect of the Aryan-Semitic debate that underlay so much of the century's thinking. In his poem the obsession with filiation can be seen as a way of interrogating the present in order to force it to confess to an unassimilable past.

A question that concerned many nineteenth-century writers was what to do with the Lord's gift, Hebrew monotheism, which was seen as sublime in its Christian guise but otherwise odious. Often the solution was to prove in one way or another that what was originally an unshared divine treasure became a universal gift thanks to the genius of the Aryans. The appropriation of an allegedly prestigious past was thus carried out with an eye to the future. Modes of inquiry, designations of linguistic facts, classifications of peoples and traditions—all were shaped by the conceptual tools that scholars employed.

The circuits of knowledge were jammed. Instantaneous monotheism, which was not the product of any deliberate act of invention, strictly prohibited the Semite from communicating. This truth without images, sealed up in a name whose vowels were invisible, therefore needed an intermediary, a mediator, a Messiah whose divine body was also an overt utterance, a decipherable truth inscribed in its own unique history.[12]

Notes

1. Archives of Paradise

1. Augustine, *De civitate dei contra paganos*, 16.11.1ff.
2. Theodoret of Cyrrhus, *In loca difficilia scripturae sacrae: quaestiones selectae. In Genesin* 60–61, ed. J.-L. Schulze (Paris, 1864), col. 165–168 (J.-P. Migne, *Patrologia Greca*, 80, 1). Gregory of Nyssa, *Contra Eunomium*, ed. W. Jaeger, II, 236ff (p. 295ff) and II, 256ff (p. 301ff) (Leyden, 1960), corresponding to book XII in Migne, *Patrologia Greca*, 45, 2, 1863, col. 989ff and col. 997ff.
3. On these questions, A. Borst, *Der Turmbau von Babel: Geschichte der Meinungen über Ursprung und Vielfalt der Sprachen und Völker*, vols. 1–4 (Stuttgart, 1957–1963), remains a mine of invaluable information.
4. Simon Simplex [Andreas Kempe], *Die Sprachen des Paradises . . . In einer Rede von etlichen Hochgelehrten Persohnen . . . zusammen geschrieben von Simon Simplex . . . Aus dem Schwedischen im Teutschen übersetzt von Albrecht Kopman* (Hamburg, 1688). The Swedish original (if one existed) is unknown. Borst says that he never found one in any German library (Borst, *Der Turmbau*, vol. 3, 1, 1960, pp. 1338–1339). I consulted the copy in the Kungliga Biblioteket in Stockholm, where it is catalogued as F 1700/1679. Further information may be found in C. C. Elert, "Andreas Kempe (1622–1689) and the Languages Spoken in Paradise," *Historiographia linguistica* 5:3 (1978):221–226.
5. Kempe, *Die Sprache*, pp. 27, 28–31. On these two writers see J. Svenbro, "L'idéologie 'gothisante' et l'*Atlantica* d'Olof Rudbeck: le mythe platonicien de l'Atlantide au service de l'Empire suédois du XVIIe siècle," *Quaderni di storia* 11 (1980):121–156.
6. G. W. Leibniz, *Nouveaux essais sur l'entendement humain* (1704; 1st

ed., Amsterdam-Leipzig, Raspe, 1765), in P. Janet, ed. *Oeuvres philosophiques* (Paris, 1900), vol. 1, pp. 238ff, and in *Brevis designatio meditationum de originibus gentium* (Berlin, 1710), pp. 5–9.

7. Leibniz, *Nouveaux essais,* p. 243. See also my research notes in M. Olender, "Genèse et développement de l'idée indo-européenne," *Résumés de conférences et travaux: annuaire de l'Ecole pratique des hautes études. Section des sciences religieuses* 94(1985–1986):397–406; 95(1986–1987):142–144;96(1987–1988):125–128.

8. Better known as Goropius Becanus, he is the author of *Origines antwerpianae* (Antwerp, 1569). G. J. Metcalf writes about him in "The Indo-European Hypothesis in the Sixteenth and Seventeenth Centuries," in Dell H. Hymes, ed., *Studies in the History of Linguistics: Traditions and Paradigms* (London-Bloomington, 1974), pp. 241–245.

9. Leibniz, *Nouveaux essais,* p. 243. Van Gorp links the Cimbres to the Cimmerians (whom he considers to have been the founders of Antwerp) and to the family of Japhet, whose first son is named Gomer (Gen. 10:2). Metcalf, "The Indo-European Hypothesis," details some of Van Gorp's fabulous etymologies.

10. For information on the Scythian hypothesis and the origins of linguistics, see the innovative book by D. Droixhe, *La linguistique et l'appel de l'histoire (1600–1800): rationalisme et révolutions positivistes* (Geneva-Paris, 1978), pp. 86–89 and 126–142, and P. Swiggers, "Adrianus Schrieckius: de la langue des Scythes à l'Europe linguistique," in D. Droixhe, ed., "La genèse du comparatisme indo-européen," special issue of *Histoire, Epistémologie, Langage* 6:2 (1984):17–35. On Celtomania and the national awakening of the sixteenth century, see C. G. Dubois, *Celtes et Gaulois au XVIe siècle: le développement littéraire d'un mythe nationaliste* (Paris, 1972), which contains a critical edition of an unpublished treatise by Guillaume Postel, *De ce qui est premier pour réformer le monde.*

11. See, most recently, the work of two Soviet scholars, T. V. Gamkrelidze and V. V. Ivanov, *Indoevropejskij jazyk i Indoevropejcy: rekonstrukcija i istorikotipologiceskij analiz prajazyka i protkultury* (The Indo-European language and the Indo-Europeans: historical-typological reconstruction and analysis of the original language and protoculture), with a preface by Roman Jakobson (Tbilisi, 1984), 2 vols.

Part of the introduction to this work was translated into French by B. Paritakine: "Système de langue et principes de reconstruction en linguistique," *Diogène* 137 (1987):3–23. See also G. Charachidzé, "Gamq'relize/Ivanov, les Indo-Europeéns et le Caucase," *Revue des études georgiennes et caucasiennes* 2 (1986):211–222, together with his review in *Bulletin de la Société de linguistique de Paris* 81:2 (1986):97–112.

12. Richard Simon, *Histoire critique du Vieux Testament* (1678; Rotterdam, 1685), p. 85.

13. Ibid., p. 487. See also D. S. Katz, *Philo-Semitism and the Readmission of the Jews to England, 1603–1655* (Oxford, 1982), especially pp. 65ff.

14. Simon, *Histoire critique*, p. 84, for this and the following citations. Citations without page references are to the same page as the previous citation.

15. J. G. Herder, *Vom Geist der ebraïschen Poesie* I(1782), ed. B. Suphan (Berlin, 1879), vol. 11, pp. 444–445.

16. J. G. Herder, *Ideen zur Philosophie der Geschichte der Menschheit (1784–1791)*, ed. B. Suphan (Berlin, 1887), vol. 13, p. 432. On Herder and India, see R. Gérard, *L'orient et la pensée romantique allemande* (Paris, 1963), pp. 12ff, 40–41, and 47ff; A. L. Wilson, *A Mythical Image: The Ideal of India in German Romanticism* (Durham, 1964), pp. 50ff.

17. Herder, *Ideen*, vol. 13, pp. 431 and 432.

18. Among other possible examples is P. D. Huet, *Traité de la situation du Paradis terrestre* (1691), recently studied by J.-R. Massimi in A. Desreumaux and F. Schmidt, eds., *Moïse géographe: recherches sur les représentations juives et chrétiennes de l'espace* (Paris, 1988), pp. 203–225. C. Malte-Brun (1775–1826) examined the state of the question in 1811 in "Digression sur l'Eden et le Paradis terrestre," in *Précis de la géographie universelle* (Paris, 1811), vol. 3, pp. 245–248. On the location of Paradise see M. Alexandre, "Entre ciel et terre: les premiers débats sur le site du Paradis (Genèse 2:8–15 et ses réceptions)," in F. Jouan and B. Deforge, eds., *Peuples et pays mythiques* (Paris, 1988), pp. 187–224.

19. Ernest Renan, *Oeuvres complètes*, ed. H. Psichari, vol. 8, p. 238.

20. In the second half of the nineteenth century, see for example the

discussion below of the debate between Darwin and F. Max Müller. For a bibliography on the origins of language, see G. W. Hewes, *Language Origins: A Bibliography,* 2nd ed., revised and augmented (The Hague-Paris, 1975), 2 vols. See also Borst, *Der Turmbau.*

21. J. G. Herder, *Abhandlung über den Ursprung der Sprache* (1770), ed. B. Suphan (Berlin, 1891), vol. 5, p. 52: "Und was ist also die ganze Bauart der Sprache anders, als eine Entwickelungsweise seines Geistes, eine Geschichte seiner Entdeckungen!"

22. Leibniz, *Nouveaux essais,* pp. 294 and 242.

23. In 1759 this dissertation was honored with a prize awarded by the Prussian Royal Academy of Sciences and Belles Lettres. The quotation is from pp. 28–29 of the French edition, published in Bremen in 1762, which was revised and enlarged by the author.

24. E. B. de Condillac, *Essai sur l'origine des connaissances humaines* (1746), II, 1 of chapter XV, "Du génie des langues," (Paris: G. Le Roy, 1947),pp. 103, 98. On the importance of Condillac in these debates, see Hans Aarsleff, "The Tradition of Condillac: The Problem of the Origin of Language in the Eighteenth Century and the Debate in the Berlin Academy before Herder," in Dell H. Hymes, ed., *Studies in the History of Linguistics: Traditions and Paradigms* (London-Bloomington, 1974), pp. 93–156, rept. in Aarsleff, *From Locke to Saussure: Essays on the Study of Language and Intellectual History* (London, 1982), pp. 146–209.

25. Wilhelm von Humboldt (1767–1835) proposed a subtle analysis of the dynamic relations between language and national character in his *Latium und Hellas oder Betrachtungen über das classische Alterthum* (1806), vol. 2 of *Werke in Fünf Bänden: Schriften zur Altertumskunde und Asthetik die Vasken,* ed. A. Flitner and K. Giel, Wissenschaftliche Buchgesellschaft (Stuttgart, 1961), pp. 58ff, and in *Über die Verschiedenheit des menschlichen Sprachbaues* (1830–1835), vol. 3 of *Werke: Schriften zur Sprachphilosophie* (Stuttgart, 1963), pp. 557ff. This edition includes references to the pagination of Humboldt, *Gesammelte Schriften* (Berlin, 1903–1936), a seventeen-volume compendium of Humboldt's work published by the Berlin Academy.

26. Ferdinand de Saussure, *Cours de linguistique générale* (1910–1911), ed. T. de Mauro (Paris, 1985), p. 310. Language and race and ethnicity are discussed on pp. 304–312.

27. Saussure, *Cours,* pp. 306–310, offers an overview of "linguistic paleontology."

28. In a letter to P. Russel dated September 8, 1785, Jones expresses his "hopes of learning the rudiments of this venerable [language]," and a few weeks letter, in an October dispatch to Sir J. Macpherson, he announces that he has "just begun" the study of Sanskrit. See G. Cannon, ed., *The Letters of Sir William Jones* (Oxford, 1970), vol. 2, pp. 680 and 687.

29. William Jones, "On the Hindus: The Third Discourse," *Asiatic Researches* 1 (1799):422–423. French translation in *Recherches asiatiques ou Mémoires de la Société établie au Bengale,* 1, revised, with supplementary notes by Langlès, Cuvier, Delambre, Lamarck, and Olivier, translated from the English by A. Labaume (Paris, 1805), pp. 508–509. For the philological impact of Jones's work, see Hans Aarsleff, *The Study of Language in England, 1780–1860* (Princeton, 1967), pp. 115–161.

30. See B. Hemmerdinger, "La théorie irano-germanique de Juste Lipse (1598)," *Indogermanische Forschungen* 76 (1971):20–21; J. Fellman, "The First Comparative Indo-Europeanist," *Linguistics* 145 (1975):83–85; J. F. Eros, "A 17th-Century Demonstration of Language Relationship: Meric Casaubon on English and Greek," *Historiographia linguistica* 3:1 (1976):1–13; J. C. Muller, "Forschungsbericht: Early Stages of Language Comparison from Sassetti to Sir William Jones (1786)," *Kratylos* 31 (1986):1–31.

31. For the context in which this essay was written, see R. Gérard, *L'orient et la pensée romantique allemande* (Paris, 1963), pp. 111ff.

32. Sylvain Lévi, "Les origines d'une chaire: l'entrée du sanscrit au Collège de France," in *Le Collège de France (1530–1930)* (Paris, 1932), pp. 329–344.

33. Or perhaps in 1820: compare M.-L. Rostaert, "Etymologie et idéologie: des reflets du nationalisme sur la lexicologie allemande, 1830–1914," *Historiographia linguistica* 6:3 (1979):309.

34. Friedrich Max Müller, *Nouvelles leçons sur la science du langage* (1863), translated from the English by G. Harris and G. Perrot (Paris, 1868), vol. 2, pp. 136–137.

35. See below, and D. S. Hawley, "L'Inde de Voltaire," in T. Besterman, ed., *Studies on Voltaire and the Eighteenth Century* 120 (1974):139–

178. See also C. Weinberger-Thomas, "Les mystères du Veda: spéculations sur le texte sacré des anciens brames du siècle des Lumières," *Purusartha* 7 (1983):177–231.
36. *Journal de Genève,* April 17, 1878, p. 3, col. 1.
37. Ibid.
38. Salomon Reinach, *L'origine des Aryens: histoire d'une controverse* (Paris, 1892), p. 19. Based on lectures given at the Ecole du Louvre in 1891, this book was published in the year of the death of Renan, whom Reinach does not cite.
39. J. Darmesteter, "Rapport annuel," *Journal asiatique,* 1890, p. 25.
40. See Sylvain Lévi, *La grande encyclopédie* (1885–1902), vol. 4, p. 46, "Aryens II. Linguistique."
41. G. W. F. Hegel, *Philosophie der Weltgeschichte,* II, 2. *Die griechische und römische Welt,* in *Sämtliche Werke,* ed. G. Lasson (Leipzig, 1923), vol. 9, p. 728.
42. The first sentence is taken from fragments written in Hegel's own hand. The portion in brackets is based on student notebooks used in the compilation of the text. The remainder is from Hegel, *Die Vernunft in der Geschichte* (1830; 1st ed. 1837), ed. J. Hoffmeister (Berlin: Akademie Verlag, 1966), pp. 158–159. [The English translation is adapted from Hegel, *Reason in History,* trans. Robert S. Hartman (New York: Liberal Arts Press, 1953), p. 72.—Tr.] On Hegel and India, see M. Hulin, *Hegel et l'Orient, suivi de la traduction annotée d'un essai de Hegel sur la Bhagavad-Gita* (Paris, 1979), pp. 99–124; Roger-Pol Droit, *L'oubli de l'Inde: une amnésie philosophique* (Paris, 1989), pp. 195–207.
43. Lévi, *Encyclopédie.* See Chapter 5 for Max Müller's use of linguistic roots.
44. For some scholars, the Indians of the Veda took the place of the Old Testament Jews. Pierre Vidal-Naquet has shown how one magical continent can take the place of another in the case of the philological reconstruction of Atlantis: see his "Hérodote et l'Atlantide: entre les Grecs et les Juifs. Réflexions sur l'historiographie du siècle des Lumières," *Quaderni di storia* 16 (1982):5–74, and "L'Atlantide et les nations," *Représentations de l'origine: littérature, histoire, civilisation. Cahiers du Centre de recherches littéraires et historiques et du Centre de recherches Afro-Indien-Océaniques de l'université de la Réunion* 4 (1987):9–28.

45. The first, more or less abstract, technical use of older meanings for the term Aryan may be in A. H. Anquetil-Duperron (1731–1805), "Recherches sur les anciennes langues de la Perse: premier mémoire sur le zend" (August 9, 1763), *Mémoires de littérature, tirés des registres de l'Académie royale des inscriptions et belles-lettres* 31 (1768):370 and note 24, pp. 389–390. Hans Siegert deserves credit for his courage in publishing, in Germany in 1941, an article on the uses and abuses of the term: "Zur Geschichte der Begriffe 'Arier' und 'arisch,'" *Wörter und Sachen* 22 (1941–42):73–99. For the new use of the term Aryan attributed to Anquetil, compare Siegert, pp. 86–87, with K. Koerner, "Observations on the Sources, Transmission, and Meaning of 'Indo-European' and Related Terms in the Development of Linguistics," in K. Koerner, ed., *Papers from the Third International Conference on Historical Linguistics* (Amsterdam, 1982), p. 169. On the exact use of the term today, see G. Charachidzé, *La mémoire indo-européenne du Caucase* (Paris, 1987), pp. 133–136.

46. Its introduction long attributed to J. von Klaproth (1783–1835) in 1823, the term Indo-German was used in 1810 by C. Malte-Brun, *Précis de la géographie universelle* (Paris, 1810), vol. 2, pp. 577–581. See F. R. Shapiro, "On the Origin of the Term 'Indo-Germanic,'" *Historiographia linguistica* 8:1 (1981):165–170.

47. In an anonymous review of J. C. Adelung, *Mithridates, oder Allgemeine Sprachenkunde* (Berlin, 1806–1812) attributed by Siegert ("Zur Geschichte," pp. 75–76) to T. Young, the author proposes the term "Indoeuropean": *The Quarterly Review* 10 (Oct. 1813–Jan. 1814):255; see also pp. 256, 264, 270, 273, and 281. See the review article by Koerner, "Observations," pp. 153–180, which discusses the arguments of F. R. Shapiro, reprinted in *Practicing Linguistic Historiography: Selected Essays* (Amsterdam-Philadelphia, 1989), pp. 149–178).

48. In 1848, in the first version of his *Origine du langage*, Renan wrote "Indo-Germanic languages" (*La liberté de penser* 13 [Dec. 1848]:68), whereas later he chose "Indo-European" (*Oeuvres complètes*, vol. 8, pp. 71–72). But later in the same work, on p. 211, he reverts to "Indo-Germanic."

49. This old denomination was revived in the 1920s in the Soviet Union owing to the "Japhetic theory" of N. J. Marr (1865–1934). See R. L'Hermitte, *Science et perversion idéologique: Marr, marrisme, marristes.*

Une page de l'histoire de la linguistique soviétique, "Cultures et Sociétés de l'Est," 8 (Paris, 1987).

50. "Arian" was the choice of Adolphe Pictet. See Chapter 6.

51. I use variable terminology in paraphrasing the various texts examined in this book. Thus I may write Indo-European, Aryan, Arian, or Indo-German, depending on the author I am examining, and without enclosing the words in quotation marks.

52. A. L. von Schlözer explicitly proposed applying the formula "Semitic" to the languages of "Syrians, Babylonians, Hebrews, and Arabs": "Von den Chaldäern," *Repertorium für biblische und morgenländische Litteratur* 8 (1781):161; Herder used the terms "Semite" and "Semitic" in the first part of his treatise on *L'esprit de la poésie hébraïque* (Berlin: R. Suphan, 1879), vol. 11, pp. 429, 442–444; the preface is dated April 9, 1782.

53. Franz Bopp, *Grammaire comparée des langues indo-européennes* (1833–1849), trans. from the German by M. Bréal (Paris, 1866), vol. 1, p. 21.

54. Georges Dumézil, *Leçon inaugurale à la chaire de civilisation indo-européenne du Collège de France,* delivered on December 1, 1949 (Paris, 1950), pp. 6–7.

55. E. Renan, *Oeuvres,* vol. 8, p. 578. A.-A. Cournot (1801–1877), a reader of Renan who had studied widely in many areas, developed similar ideas. He saw the Indo-European and Semitic families as sharing the "same or neighboring cradles" at the birthplace of civilization. See Cournot, *Traité de l'enchaînement des idées fondamentales dans les sciences et dans l'histoire* (1861; Paris, 1922), pp. 623ff.

56. By way of example, see the long excerpt from Pictet cited in the last section of Chapter 6.

57. "Jede Epoche is unmittelbar zu Gott." Leopold von Ranke, *Über die Epochen der neueren Geschichte: Vorträge dem Könige Maximilian II. von Bayern gehalten* (1854; 1st ed. 1888; Darmstadt, 1982), p. 7. See also I. Meyerson, "Le temps, la mémoire, l'histoire" (1956), in *Ecrits, 1921–1983: pour une psychologie historique* (Paris, 1987), pp. 274ff.

58. Edgar Quinet, introduction to J. G. Herder, *Idées sur la philosophie de l'histoire de l'humanité,* trans. from the German by E. Quinet (Paris, 1827), vol. 1, pp. 10ff and pp. 60ff.

59. I have learned a great deal on this subject from Paul Bénichou, *Le temps des prophètes: doctrines de l'âge romantique* (Paris, 1977), and *Les mages romantiques* (Paris, 1988).

60. Meyerson, "Le temps," pp. 271–272.

61. "Today, even though the genius of analysis and skepticism seem to have changed everything, we have no other historical belief. Only what was particular has become general. What had been palpable has become intangible. What had appeared in one place and one time has become the work of all places and all times." Quinet, in Herder, *Idées,* p. 10.

62. See in this connection G. E. Lessing's *Nathan der Weise* (1779), particularly the parable of the three rings in Act 3.

63. J. Pommier, *La jeunesse cléricale d'Ernest Renan-Saint-Sulpice* (Strasburg, 1933), pp. 122ff and 519ff.

64. Michel Foucault, *Les mots et les choses: une archéologie des sciences humaines* (1966; Paris, 1981), p. 294.

65. P. B. Salmon, "The Beginnings of Morphology: Linguistic Botanizing in the 18th Century," *Historiographia linguistica* 1:3 (1974):313–339; K. Koerner, "Schleichers Einfluss auf Haeckel: Schlaglichter auf die wechselseitige Abhängigkeit zwischen linguistischen und biologischen Theorien im 19. Jahrhundert," *Zeitschrift für vergleichende Sprachforschung* 95 (1981):3–21.

66. Ferdinand de Saussure, *Cours de linguistique générale* (1910–1911), ed. T. de Mauro (Paris, 1985), p. 16.

67. *Le Journal de Genève,* April 19, 1878, p. 3, col. 1.

68. Saussure, *Cours,* p. 17.

69. As indicated by recent discussions of the work of Gamkrelidze and Ivanov; see Note 11.

70. On Michelet as "theologian," see Bénichou, *Le Temps,* p. 552.

71. "Orientation des recherches et projets d'enseignement, présentés par Alexandre Koyré à l'Assemblée des professeurs du Collège de France" (March 11, 1951), in Alexandre Koyré, *De la mystique à la science: cours, conférences et documents, 1922–1962* (Paris, 1986), p. 129.

72. See Georges Canguilhem, *Etudes d'histoire et de philosophie des sciences* (Paris, 1983), pp. 20–23, which makes the same point with reference to Koyré.

73. Léon Poliakov, *Le mythe aryen: essai sur les sources du racisme et des nationalismes* (Paris, 1971).
74. See C. Guillaumin, *L'idéologie raciste: Genèse et langage actuel* (Paris, 1972), and, more recently, among many other works, R. Römer, *Sprachwissenschaft und Rassenideologie in Deutschland* (Munich, 1985); P.-A. Taguieff, *La force du préjugé: essai sur le racisme et ses doubles* (Paris, 1988); Julia Kristeva, *Etrangers à nous-mêmes* (Paris, 1988); Tzvetan Todorov, *Nous et les autres: la réflexion française sur la diversité humaine* (Paris, 1989).
75. Goldziher lived until 1921, but we are concerned with his book on Hebrew mythology, published in 1876. While Renan, Max Müller, and Pictet helped to develop new sciences, they also spread the Aryan idea to the general public. Goldziher also hoped to reach a nonspecialist audience with his response to their work. Richard Wagner (1813–1883), for example, drew on contemporary scholarship to exploit both the lyrical and the political aspects of Aryanism.
76. The title of my original seminar at the Ecole des Hautes Etudes en Sciences Sociales in 1985 was "Les langues du Paradis: question d'historiographie indo-européenne."

2. Divine Vowels

1. Letter 7 of Jean Domenge, October 25, 1723, published in J. Dehergne and D. D. Leslie, *Juifs de Chine à travers la correspondance inédite des jésuites du dix-huitième siècle* (Paris-Rome, 1984), p. 162. Domenge, remarking on what he considered the incredible fact that "they have absolutely no knowledge of the Messiah," wrote in the same letter: "But I prefer to think that, having had such knowledge, they later lost it" (p. 163). On the Jewish community of K'ai-feng, see J. Preuss, *The Chinese Jews of Kaifeng-Fu* (Tel Aviv, 1961). For a recent report on Chinese who claim to be descendants of that community, see K. Alfonsi, *Le Nouvel Observateur* 1237 (July 22, 1988):32–33.
2. In the preface ("Epistre") by Charles Le Gobien to vol. 7 of *Lettres édifiantes et curieuses, écrites des missions étrangères, par quelques missionaires de la Compagnie de Jésus,* 1707. The *Journal des Sçavans* cited above reviewed this volume.

3. This was the answer given by the Chinese Jews when Father Domenge asked them "why their ancient Bible was not punctuated" (see Letter 7, cited in note 1).

4. On verbal and nonverbal inspiration, see E. Mangenot, "Inspiration de l'Ecriture," *Dictionnaire de théologie catholique,* vol. 7, 2 (1923), cols. 2192ff. In the context that concerns us, see E. Renan, "L'exégèse biblique et l'esprit français," *Revue des Deux Mondes* 60:6 (1865):238; E. Cassirer, *La philosophie des lumières* (Paris, 1966), p. 195 [*The Philosophy of the Enlightenment* (Princeton: Princeton University Press, 1951)]; P. Auvray, *Richard Simon (1638–1712)* (Paris, 1974), p. 92; M. Hadas-Lebel, "Le père Houbigant et la critique textuelle," in Y. Belaval and D. Bourel, eds., *Le siècle des lumières et la bible* (Paris, 1986), p. 105; F. Laplanche, "La Bible chez les réformés," ibid., pp. 469–470.

5. References are to the Rotterdam edition of 1685, revised by the author.

6. In a letter to M. de Malézieu dated May 19, 1702, *Correspondance* (Paris, 1920), vol. 13, p. 309. Concerning the condemnation of the *Critical History* and its author, see J. Steinmann, *Richard Simon et les origines de l'exégèse biblique* (Bruges, 1960), pp. 124–130; M. Rodinson, "Richard Simon et la dédogmatisation," *Les Temps Modernes* 202 (March 1963):1700–1709; Auvray, *Richard Simon,* p. 47, n. 2; pp. 67–68, 76–79. It is known from Leibniz's correspondence that he followed this controversy. See J. Le Brun, "Entre la *Perpétuité* et la *Demonstratio Evangelica," Leibniz à Paris (1672–1676)* (Wiesbaden, 1978), vol. 2, p. 7, n. 62.

7. For the influence of Spinoza and Simon on biblical exegesis, see Renan, "L'exégèse biblique," pp. 239–240, and *Oeuvres complètes,* vol. 7, pp. 827–828; Steinmann, *Richard Simon,* pp. 50–53; P. Auvray, "Richard Simon and Spinoza," *Religion, érudition et critique à la fin du XVIIe siècle et au début du XVIIIe* (Paris, 1968), pp. 201–214; Auvray, *Richard Simon,* pp. 42–43 and 64–66. Simon, who had several of Spinoza's works in his library (see ibid., pp. 207–208), expresses his disagreement with the author of the *Tractatus theologico-politicus* (1670) at several points in the preface of his *Histoire critique* (1678).

8. Spinoza, *Abrégé de grammaire hébraique,* ed. J. Askénazi and J. Askénazi-Gerson (Paris, 1968), pp. 35–36.

9. On the dating of this text, see A. Dotan, "Masorah," *Encyclopedia judaica,* vol. 16 (1971), cols. 1416–1417.

10. The image of "melody" is from Zohar, cited in Spinoza, *Abrégé,* p. 35, n. 1. The dispute over the dating of the vowel signs was revived by Louis Cappel (1585–1658), who published his *Arcanum punctationis revelatum* in Leyden in 1624. For Simon's view, see *Histoire critique,* pp. 475–481. Further details in M. Hadas-Lebel, "Les études hébraïques en France au XVIIIe siècle et la création de la première chaire d'Ecriture sainte en Sorbonne," *Revue des études juives* 144:1–3 (1985):93–126; M. Hadas-Lebel, "Le père Houbigant et la critique textuelle," in Belaval and Bourel, eds., *Le siècle des lumières,* pp. 107–112; F. Laplanche, "La bible chez les réformés," ibid., pp. 463–466; B. E. Schwarzbach, "L'*Encyclopédie* de Diderot et de d'Alembert," ibid., pp. 772–773. For the views of the Church Fathers, especially Jerome, on the Hebrew vowels, see J. Barr, "St. Jerome's Appreciation of Hebrew," *Bulletin of the John Rylands Library* 49:2 (1967):281–302; J. Barr, "St. Jerome and the Sounds of Hebrew," *Journal of Semitic Studies* 12:1 (1967):1–36. Louis Massignon has also meditated on the inspiration contained in the vowels of the Semitic languages: "La syntaxe intérieure des langues sémitiques et le mode de recueillement qu'elles inspirent" (1949), in *Opera minora* (Beirut, 1963), vol. 2, pp. 570–580; "Voyelles sémitiques et sémantique musicale" (1956), ibid., pp. 638–642. In a different context, see the chapter on the "world of the vowel" by Michel de Certeau in Michel de Certeau, Dominique Julia, and Jacques Revel, eds., *Une politique de la langue: la révolution française et les patois* (Paris, 1975), pp. 110–121.

11. Mangenot, "Inspiration," col. 2192.

12. Simon, *Histoire critique,* preface. On divine inspiration, see note 5. For Origen's views, see F. Schmidt, "L'écriture falsifiée," *Le Temps de la réflexion* 5 (1984):159–161. See also Steinmann, *Richard Simon,* pp. 100ff. Further details are in J. Le Brun, "Das Entstehen der historischen Kritik im Bereich der religiösen Wissenschaften im 17. Jahrhundert," *Trierer theologische Zeitschrift* 89:2 (1980):107ff; J. Le Brun, "La réception de la théologie de Grotius chez les catholiques de la seconde moitié du XVIIe siècle," *The World of Hugo Grotius (1583–1645)* (Amsterdam-Maarssen, 1984), pp. 195ff and 203ff.

On the hypothesis of the scribes in Simon, the "public writers or prophets who recorded the most important events in the republic of the Hebrews," see his preface and pp. 15ff. See also M. Yardeni, "La vision des juifs et du judaïsme dans l'oeuvre de Richard Simon," *Revue des études juives* 129:24 (1970):188ff.

13. For an example of the tension between divine inspiration and accuracy of the text two centuries later, see E. Poulat, *Critique et mystique: autour de Loisy ou la conscience catholique et l'esprit moderne* (Paris, 1984), pp. 14–43. One day in the summer of 1881, Louis Duchesne lent Alfred Loisy a volume of the Tischendorf edition of the Gospels. The young Hebrew professor then began comparing different versions of the resurrection of Christ. "It was clear to me that the differences affected the fundamental meaning of the texts, but I did not draw the ultimate consequences of my findings. I concluded that although divine inspiration guaranteed the truth of Scripture, it did not guarantee accuracy of detail, even on very important points" (p. 18). On inspiration in the Bible, modernists, and Loisy, see Mangenot, "Inspiration," cols. 2191–2192, 2202, 2255, and 2264.

14. On Walton's "polyglot Bible" see Steinmann, *Richard Simon,* pp. 117–123. For the ideas of "original" and "authentic" in Simon and their relevance to debates between Catholics and Protestants, see J. Le Brun, "Sens et portée du retour aux origines dans l'oeuvre de Richard Simon," *XVIIe Siècle* 33:2 (1981):185–198.

15. On the status of the Bible as text in the seventeenth century, see Michel de Certeau, "L'idée de traduction de la bible au XVIIe siècle: Sacy et Simon," *Recherches de science religieuse* 66:1 (1978):73–92. On the reception of Simon's work, see B. E. Schwarzbach, "La fortune de Richard Simon au XVIIIe siècle," *Revue des études juives* 146:1–2 (1987):225–239.

16. *De sacra poesi hebraeorium praelectiones* (Oxford, 1753). An English-language edition, *Lectures on the Sacred Poetry of the Hebrews,* appeared in 1787. Citations in the text are from the first French edition, published in Lyons in 1812. [These passages have been retranslated into English from the French.—Tr.] Lowth's treatise was translated into many European languages.

17. In the original Latin, Lowth used *sublimis* and related words (*sublim-*

itas, etc.). Lectures 14–17 are concerned with the sublime and the sacred poets. Drawing on an ancient tradition, Lowth refers to the *Peri hupsous*, a brief treatise *On the Sublime*, long attributed to Longinus and translated into French by Boileau in 1674 (pp. 297–298, 317). In *Peri hupsous* (IX, 9), the biblical *fiat lux* is one of the examples of the sublime. For recent reflections on this theme, see M. Deguy, ed., *Du sublime* (Paris, 1988).

18. In the Latin edition consulted, published in Göttingen, 1770, p. 307.

19. These images are from Lowth. He says that in order to read the Hebrew text one must "in some sense imitate the [comparative] method of the astronomers . . . moving from one planet to another and becoming, for a few moments, inhabitants of each" (pp. 98 and 90–91 of the Latin edition).

20. On p. 90 of the Latin edition.

21. In *A Sermon Preached at the Visitation of the Honourable and Right Reverend Richard Lord Bishop of Durham* (London, 1758), Lowth holds that Christianity must henceforth be studied "as a science and an art" (p. 7), which implies "the free exercise of reason and private judgment" (p. 15). This sermon is singled out by F. Deconinck-Brossard, "L'Ecriture dans la prédication anglaise," in Belaval and Bourel, eds., *Le siècle des lumières*, p. 542.

22. Lowth, *Sermon*, p. 16, for this and subsequent quotes.

23. All references to Herder are to the B. Suphan edition, thirty-three volumes published in Berlin between 1877 and 1913. Where no volume number is specified, the page refers to the same volume as the previous reference.

24. Between 1762 and 1764 Herder studied in Königsberg, where he encountered these two teachers. See Isaiah Berlin, *Vico and Herder: Two Studies in the History of Ideas* (London, 1976), pp. 165–167; and A. Philonenko, *La théorie kantienne de l'histoire* (Paris, 1986), pp. 125ff.

25. For the Egyptians and Indians, for example, see *Auch eine Philosophie* (1774), 1891, vol. 5, pp. 487ff and 497; *Ideen zur Philosophie* (1784–1791), 1909, vol. 14, pp. 28ff.

26. G. Cannon, "Sir William Jones, Persian, Sanskrit and the Asiatic Society," *Histoire, Epistémologie, Langage* 6:2 (1984):83–94.

27. "Die Sprache des Paradieses." *Vom Geist der ebraïschen Poesie* I, 1782, vol. 11, p. 444. The subsequent citations are from pp. 444–445.

28. Vol. 5, p. 87. Herder frequently brings these two notions together, as on ibid., p. 70. Subsequent citations are from pp. 13–14. On this treatise, which won the prize offered by the Berlin Academy of Sciences in the spring of 1771, and on the context in which it was written, see E. Sapir, "Herder's *Ursprung der Sprache*" (1905), *Historiographia linguistica* 11:3 (1984):355–388. See also Aarsleff, *From Locke to Saussure.*

29. Herder wrote Eutyphron rather than Euthyphron. In Greek the adjective *euthiphron* means "with righteous heart, benevolent" and *alciphron* means "with courage, bellicose."

30. Herder had already made this point in his preface. On the idea that the cruder and more primitive a language is, the more powerful its expression of feeling, see Herder's *Ursprung der Sprache* (1772), vol. 5, pp. 70–71, 78, 82–83, 87. Concerning the priority of poetry over prose and the idea that the poorer the culture, the richer the poetry, and the belief in poetry as the original form of human expression, see M. Rouché, *La philosophie de l'histoire de Herder* (Paris, 1940), pp. 15ff.

31. Elsewhere the human being is called "a creature of language": *Ein Geschöpf der Sprache*, pp. 93 and 69.

32. Herder is quite explicit on this point in his *Christliche Schriften* (1798), vol. 20, p. 48, when he says that the expression "Spirit of God" does not mean that men inspired with that spirit resonate like "an organ pipe through which air is blown" nor that they are like "a hollow machine" without ideas of their own.

3. The Cycle of the Chosen Peoples

1. In 1778 Herder raised the question of the effects of a people's poetry on its customs in *Über die Wirkung der Dichtkunst auf die Sitten der Völker in alten und neuen Zeiten,* vol. 8, pp. 334–436. One section, pp. 344–365, is devoted to Hebrew poetry.

2. Vol. 10, p. 139; vol. 17, p. 285. For a discussion of Herder's social and political thought, barely touched on here, see F. M. Barnard,

"The Hebrews and Herder's Political Creed," *The Modern Language Review* 54:4 (1959):539ff, 545; F. M. Barnard, *Herder's Social and Political Thought: From Enlightenment to Nationalism* (Oxford, 1965), pp. 55ff and 72ff; F. M. Barnard, "Herder and Israel," *Jewish Social Studies* 28:1 (1966):25–33; Isaiah Berlin, *Vico and Herder: Two Studies in the History of Ideas* (London, 1976), pp. 180ff.

3. Herder elsewhere expressed his wariness of anachronism. In the *Frankfurter gelehrten Anzeigen* of April 28, 1772, he published a critical review of the first two (of six) volumes of *Mosaiches Recht* (1770–1775) by J. D. Michaelis, who, according to Herder, treated the Jewish state as a "winged, poetic republic," as if it were "the celebrated island of Atlantis" (vol. 5, p. 424). He also criticized Michaelis for imputing modern commonplaces to the historical Moses and of portraying a democratic nation as "a luminous Utopia hovering between heaven and earth" (p. 425).

4. Twenty-six years after publishing the *Beobachtungen über das Gefühl des Schönen und Erhabenen* (1764) [*Kants Gesammelte Schriften* (Berlin, 1905), vol. 2, pp. 205–256], Kant referred to the commandment "Thou shalt make no graven image or idol" (repeated several times in the Bible, including Exodus 20:4) as "the most sublime passage in the Jews' book of laws." *Kritik der Urtheilskraft* (1790) [*Kants Gesammelte Schriften*, vol. 5, p. 274]. This was Kant's way of expressing his admiration for the Jews' powers of abstraction.

5. Herder included a highly critical chapter about the Jews from a very different perspective in the third part of his *Ideas* (1787) (vol. 14, pp. 58ff), where he tries to show that the admirable principles of the Mosaic law ended in political disaster for the people of Israel.

6. Throughout this passage Herder makes frequent use of the verbs *fühlen, einfühlen,* and *empfinden* (to feel, to empathize, to sympathize).

7. Goethe (1749–1832) wrote in his memoirs of the importance of his encounter with Herder in Strasbourg, and he left subsequent generations an idealized portrait of the man who was one of the teachers of the younger generation of Germans: *Aus meinem Leben: Dichtung und Wahrheit* (1811–1833), in *Goethes Werke,* ed. L. Blumenthal and E. Trunz, vol. 9 (1955), pp. 402ff. Elsewhere in the same autobiography Goethe wrote: "To regard the Bible as a work of compila-

tion, assembled bit by bit, reworked at various times, flattered my petty vanity insofar as this way of thinking was still far from prevalent, much less accepted in the circles in which I moved" (pp. 508–509).

8. Specifically, Herder contrasts *Fortgang* (vol. 5, pp. 511ff and 527ff) with *Fortschritt* when, in discussing "the march of human destiny," he associates *Verbesserung* (also opposed to *Fortgang*) with *Riesenschritt* (giant step) and *grosser Schritt* (large step) (vol. 5, p. 527). On the idea of progress in Herder, see M. Rouché, *La philosophie de l'histoire de Herder* (Paris, 1940), pp. 3ff, 229ff, and 542ff; Barnard, *Herder's Social and Political Thought,* pp. 128–138; Berlin, *Vico and Herder,* pp. 163ff and 186ff.

9. Herder was thoroughly familiar with Montesquieu (1689–1755), who is also cited here (vol. 4, p. 472). In *L'esprit des lois* (1748) Montesquieu wrote of the "drawbacks of transporting a religion from one country to another" (book 24, chaps. 25–26). For the influence of Montesquieu on Herder, see M. Rouché, *La philosophie de l'histoire de Herder,* pp. 21ff, and his introduction to J. G. Herder, *Journal de mon voyage en l'an 1769* (Paris, 1942), pp. 38ff.

10. Herder takes his inspiration here from Matthew 20:1–16.

11. See, for example, a text from 1797 (vol. 18, p. 248), in which Herder insists that "each nation must be considered as unique in its position" and "each people as if were the only one on earth" (p. 249). Rouché develops this idea of spiritual "autarchy" in *La philosophie de l'histoire de Herder,* pp. 34–37; in his introduction to Herder's *Journal de mon voyage en l'an 1769,* pp. 39ff and 47, and in his introduction to J. G. Herder, *Une autre philosophie de l'histoire* (Paris, 1943; rept. 1964), p. 73.

12. Herder points out that this new culture, issuing from the Ukraine, extended its borders through Hungary, part of Poland, and Russia to the Black Sea. Originating in the "Northwest," this new spirit would breathe new life into a lethargic Europe. To have situated, twice on one page, these fertile regions in the "Northwest," Herder must have been looking at a map of Eurasia or else have been thinking of the Orient.

13. Friedrich Schlegel formulated this idea in fragment 80 of the *Athenäum,* where he wrote: "Der Historiker ist ein rückwärts gekehrter

Prophet" (the historian is a backward-looking prophet). See *Athenäums-Fragmente* (1798) in *Kritische Friedrich-Schlegel-Ausgabe,* ed. E. Behler with the collaboration of J.-J. Anstett and H. Eichner (Munich, 1967), vol. 2, 1, p. 176. Concerning this "prophetic" vision of history and the influence of Hamann on young Herder, see Rouché, introduction to *Une autre philosophie,* pp. 49, 78, and 90ff.

14. In this passage of the *Briefe, das Studium der Theologie betreffend (1780–1785) zwölfter Brief* (vol. 10, pp. 139ff), in which Herder illustrates the mirror relation between Scripture and history, he gives the following formula: "Die Geschichte beweiset die Schrift, die Schrift die Geschichte" (p. 140).

15. At times Herder is clearly more theological, at times less, but they provide no basis on which to distinguish between an "early" and a "late" Herder. Certain of his writings highlight more fully than others the often contradictory tendencies of his thinking. See Rouché, *La philosophie de l'histoire,* pp. 265–266, as well as the two previously cited introductions by Rouché to French translations of Herder's work. In 1785 Kant criticized Herder for lack of "logical precision in the definition of concepts" and for the "obscurity" of his writing, which Kant considered a "philosophy of the history of humanity": *Kants Werke,* vol. 8, p. 45.

16. The pongo is one of the two varieties of orangutang distinguished by Buffon, *Histoire naturelle, générale et particulière* (Paris, 1770), vol. 12, pp. 59ff. Herder here used the Latin term *longimanus* to refer to the gibbon, with its "excessively long arms" (Buffon, ibid., p. 116).

17. See also his paean to the superiority of the temperate zone (vol. 13, p. 28, pp. 226–227).

18. On "genetic" inquiry in Herder, following Leibniz and Montesquieu, see Rouché, *La philosophie de l'histoire de Herder,* pp. 21–26; Barnard, *Herder's Social and Political Thought,* pp. 120–121.

19. Buffon, *Histoire naturelle,* vol. 5, pp. 1 and 237. Herder expressed not only moral but also physical aversion to the peoples he called Blacks and Yellows: Blacks, vol. 13, pp. 228–238; the Chinese, vol. 14, p. 8; the Japanese, vol. 13, p. 218. In 1797, however, he asserted in another context that for the natural sciences as well as the study of the natural history of humanity, there is "no hierarchy"

(keine Rangordnung) of classifications (vol. 18, p. 248). He stipulates quite explicitly that if the white looks upon the black as "a dark beast," the black has "just as much right" to look upon the white as a member of a degenerate species *(eine Abart)*.

20. He does not rule out the possibility that the stars also have an influence on physical and intellectual differences between peoples, and he expresses hope that one day astrology might be reconstituted on a scientific basis (vol. 13, pp. 31–32).

21. This way of construing the close relation between climate and politics was a commonplace of the time, derived largely from Montesquieu. See note 10 and Berlin, *Vico and Herder,* pp. 147–148.

22. But see vol. 18, p. 249, for a 1797 text in which he opposes any use of "our European culture as a general measure of goodness and human value."

23. Although opposed to philosophies of reason, Herder was often a man of the Enlightenment in spite of himself. On his deep affinities with the *Aufklärung,* of which he offered a Christian version (for example, in his *Christliche Schriften* of 1798, vol. 20, pp. 46–47), see M. Rouché, introduction to *Idées pour la philosophie de l'histoire de l'humanité* (Paris, 1962), p. 69; Barnard, *Herder's Social and Political Thought,* pp. 89ff; Berlin, *Vico and Herder,* p. 210.

24. Vol. 4, p. 472; vol. 6, pp. 74ff, 78–80, 84.

25. In the *Frankfurter gelehrten Anzeigen* for July 17, 1772 (vol. 5, p. 435). Herder is here criticizing C. Denina (1731–1813) in a review of the first volume of his *Staatsveränderungen von Italien* (Leipzig, 1771).

26. For a survey of the Augustinian tradition of Providence on which Herder drew, see A. Rascol, *Dictionnaire de théologie catholique,* vol. 13 (1936), under "La providence selon saint Augustin," cols. 961–984.

27. Vol. 7, p. 370, n. 1, B:6. For this paragraph, the editor, B. Suphan, provides details on the "draft" and "first fair copy versions" in the same volume, pp. xxx–xxxi.

28. What about his politic relations with contemporary Judaism and Jews? Herder maintained that the Jews "were and remain the most eminent people on earth . . . even in their survival today" (vol. 10, p. 139). At once hostile and conciliatory, he asserts that the Jews

are like a "parasitic plant" (vol. 14, p. 283), but that "the time will come when people in Europe will no longer ask who is Jewish and who is Christian" (p. 284). The Jews will then be assimilated and "will live according to European laws." One section of his seventh *Adrastée* of 1802 (published in the year of his death, 1803) is devoted to "the conversion of the Jews" (*Bekehrung der Juden,* vol. 24, pp. 61–75). He considered the fate of this "Asiatic people" (p. 63), foreign to Europe, not in religious terms but as "a simple question of state." While claiming that this nation, bound by Mosaic law, "belongs to Palestine and not to Europe" (p. 64) and that one day the Jews probably will return to Palestine (p. 66), Herder asserts that if one "educates the children of Jews and Christians in accordance with the principles of morality and science" (p. 75), the effect can only be to bring them together. Furthermore, "who thinks of the philosophical works of Spinoza, of Mendelssohn . . . as books written by Jews?" Finally, "their Palestine is wherever they live and work with dignity" (p. 75). Rouché tried to show how Herder was used by Nazi ideology (see the following note) in his introductions to *Une autre philosophie,* pp. 31–33 and 75–76, and *Idées,* pp. 43 and 74. Barnard saw Herder as a precursor of Herzl's Zionism (see the two articles cited in note 2).

29. On this point see the illuminating study by Hans Georg Gadamer, "Herder et ses théories sur l'histoire," *Regards sur l'histoire,* no. 2 in the *Cahiers de l'Institut allemand,* published by Karl Epting (Paris, 1941), pp. 7–36. Gadamer alludes to contemporary political events and casts Herder in the role of precursor to those "movements that are bringing new forms of political order into being today" (p. 35).

30. Berlin (*Vico and Herder,* pp. 206–211) prefers to speak of Herder's "pluralism" rather than relativism. Barnard (*Herder's Social and Political Thought,* p. 131, n. 18) stresses Herder's relativist assessment of the impact of European "progress" on other peoples.

4. *The Hebrews and the Sublime*

1. Vol. 2, p. 883. Renan was born in Tréguier in 1823 and died in Paris in 1892. In November 1882 "Le séminaire de Saint-Sulpice" appeared in the *Revue des Deux Mondes,* and in revised form it ap-

peared a year later in *Souvenirs d'enfance et de jeunesse.* Citations from Renan's works refer to *Oeuvres complètes,* ed. Henriette Psichari, 10 vols. (Paris, 1947–1961) except for a few items not included in this edition.

2. J. Pommier recounts the crucial moments in the young Renan's internal crisis in *La jeunesse cléricale d'Ernest Renan-Saint-Sulpice* (Strasbourg, 1933). On the teaching of Hebrew, see chap. 4, pp. 393ff; but see also pp. 108ff. For further information on the young Renan, see L. Rétat, *Religion et imagination religieuse: leurs formes et leurs rapports dans l'oeuvre d'Ernest Renan* (Lille, 1979), primarily part 1.

3. In using this term Renan had this in mind: "The true philologist must be at once linguist, historian, archeologist, artist, philosopher. . . . Philology is not an end in itself. Its value is as a necessary condition for the history of the human spirit and the study of the past" (vol. 3, p. 832).

4. Although philology played a part in Renan's estrangement from the Church, there is abundant evidence of the religious crisis that ended in his abandonment of the faith at Saint-Sulpice. For the year 1845, a crucial time during which he wrote his *Essai psychologique sur Jésus-Christ* (Paris, 1921), Pommer has found manuscripts in which Renan posed poignant questions concerning Christ's existence: see "L'essai psychologique de 1845," in *Un itinéraire spirituel: du séminaire à la "Prière sur l'Acropole,"* no. 4 of the *Cahiers renaniens* (Paris, 1972), pp. 25–26. In a note written in 1846 after his departure from the seminary, Renan declared himself incapable, "in the literal sense," of "imagining that there is nothing but ordinary bread in the host" (ibid., p. 23). See also Rétat, *Religion,* pp. 44–49.

5. See J. G. Herder (ed. B. Suphan, vol. 12, p. 77); L. G. A. de Bonald, *Théorie du pouvoir politique et religieux dans la société civile, démontrée par le raisonnement et par l'histoire* (1796; Paris, 1854), vol. 2, p. 98.

6. Renan, *Vie de Jésus,* vol. 4, p. 369: "Jesus of course came out of Judaism, but in the same sense that Socrates came out of the Sophist schools and Luther out of the Middle Ages." On the Hebrew people, who lacked the means to "overthrow the religion of the world and force the world to adopt their religion," see Bonald, *Théorie,* vol. 2, pp. 97–98.

7. The first draft of this work won the Volney Prize in 1847.

8. Renan frequently used "Indo-European" and "Aryan" (as well as sometimes "Indo-Germanic") interchangeably (for example, vol. 8, pp. 585–589) for both the race and the language, the two ideas being intimately related in his mind. It is important to recall the enormous influence of Eugène Burnouf (1801–1852) on historical and religious scholarship in the second half of the nineteenth century. Burnouf was an eminent Sanskritist who reconstructed Zend, the language of the Avesta.

9. Renan gave his "Discours d'ouverture du cours de langues hébraïque, chaldaïque et syriaque" at the Collège de France on February 21, 1862. The title of the first lecture was "De la part des peuples sémitiques dans l'histoire de la civilisation" (vol. 2, pp. 317–335). Four days after this first lecture, in which Renan said that Jesus was "an incomparable man" whom some "call God" (vol. 2, pp. 329–330), the Emperor suspended the course. Dismissed in 1864, Renan was replaced by Salomon Munk (1803–1867). The Collège's chair in Hebrew was given back to Renan in 1870. In 1862 he published a volume of documents concerning his dismissal along with "explanations to my colleagues" (vol. 1, pp. 143–180). Details on this whole affair can be found in H. Psichari, *Renan d'après lui-même* (Paris, 1937), pp. 224–230; R. Dussaud, *L'oeuvre scientifique d'Ernest Renan* (Paris, 1951), pp. 74–76, 119; *Un témoignage sur E. Renan: les souvenirs de I. F. A. Maury,* introduced by J. Pommier, in *Cahiers renaiens* 1 (1971):59ff and 74ff; D. Cohen, *La promotion des juifs en France à l'époque du Second Empire (1852–1870)* (Aix-en-Provence–Paris, 1980), p. 494; D. Bourel, "La *Wissenschaft des Judentums* en France," *Revue de synthèse* 2 (1988):274–277. A. Loisy recounts his memories of Renan's teaching in "L'enseignement de Renan au Collège de France," in *Le Collège de France (1530–1930)* (Paris, 1932), pp. 347–351.

10. Some held that the Semitic and Indo-European languages had common roots. Others regarded Coptic or Ghez, the ancient Ethiopian language, as the "missing link" between Semitic and Indo-European (vol.8, pp. 210ff and 430ff).

11. The expression is from Bonald, *Théorie,* vol. 2, p. 97.

12. L. G. A. Bonald, *Recherches philosophiques sur les premiers objets des*

connaissances morales (1818; Brussels, 1845), p. 153. "Unfortunate fidelity" is a leitmotif shared by many authors. Renan also attributes this intransigent fidelity to the Hebrews (vol. 7, pp. 99, 114; vol. 8, p. 147). He compares Israel's ability to preserve sacred texts with that of the Brahmins and Parsees (vol. 7, pp. 822ff).

13. See also vol. 1, pp. 272ff and 103ff.

14. "1859" is used hereafter to refer to Renan's important paper "Nouvelles considérations sur le caractère général des peuples sémitiques, et en particulier sur leur tendance au monothéisme," *Journal asiatique* (1859):214–282 and 417–450. This text was not included in Renan's *Oeuvres complètes*.

15. Another illustration of Renan's metaphorical style: "A quiver of steel arrows, a cable of stout links of twisted metal, a brass trombone rending the air with two or three sharp notes—that is Hebrew. Such a language will not express a philosophical thought or a scientific result or a doubt" (vol. 6, p. 91).

16. On the contrast between the static Semitic languages and the constantly developing Indo-European ones, see Renan, vol. 8, pp. 137, 513, 527–528, and 541.

17. For example, A.-A. Cournot (1801–1877), though he made use of raciological classifications, held in 1861 that "much work over the past century had not yielded" a definition of race. Hence there was no "precise characteristic of races that could become true entities for the naturalist." See his *Traité de l'enchaînement des idées fondamentales dans les sciences et dans l'histoire* (1861; Paris, 1922), p. 387. See also my remarks in Olender, "Racisme," in Y. Afanassiev and Marc Ferro, eds., *50 idées qui ébranlent le monde: dictionnaire de la glastnost* (Paris-Moscow, 1989).

18. Renan, who considered himself "a romantic protesting against romanticism" and a "tissue of contradictions," frequently claimed the right to contradict himself (vol. 2, p. 760). See also vol. 1, p. 552, and Psichari, *Renan d'après lui-même*, pp. 276–277.

19. See H. Laurens, "Le concept de race dans le *Journal asiatique* du XIXe siècle," *Journal asiatique* 276:3–4 (1988):371–381. Renan, one of the principal figures in the Société Asiatique, is discussed on pp. 374ff.

20. For the record, Renan always insisted on the points common to these

two indissociable branches of civilization. Among many possible examples, see vol. 8, pp. 558, 578, and 581.

21. While denying that there could be "more than one emergence *(apparition)* of the human race" (vol. 8, p. 1222), Renan did pose the question in polygenetic terms: vol. 3, p. 857; vol. 8, pp. 558, 585ff and 1222; 1859, pp. 448–449.

22. For the history of the term "civilization," see J. Moras, *Ursprung und Entwicklung des Begriffs der Zivilisation in Frankreich (1756–1830)* (Hamburg, 1930); for the identification of Christianity with civilization, see pp. 64ff. A more recent study is Jean Starobinski, "Le mot 'civilisation,'" *Le Temps de la réflexion* 4 (1983):13–51.

23. Renan discussed "linguistic races" in a lecture given at the Sorbonne on March 2, 1878, entitled "Des services rendus aux sciences historiques par la philologie" (vol. 8, pp. 1213–1232). Four years later, on March 11, 1882, he lectured, again at the Sorbonne, on "Qu'est-ce qu'une Nation?" (vol. 1, pp. 887–906). The point is that even after the Franco-Prussian War, which marked a turning point in Renan's thought, he continued to adopt different points of view on the subject of race. See also certain statements in *La réforme intellectuelle et morale* (1871).

24. Note that Renan is careful in this quote and elsewhere (e.g., 1859, p. 446) to reserve some role for blood in the transmission of cultural values, language, religion, and institutions. Similar reservations apply in contexts where Renan is denying the existence of physiological races (e.g., vol. 1, p. 456; 1859, pp. 446 and 448; vol. 6, p. 32). See also P. Gothot's analysis of "Qu'est-ce qu'une Nation?" forthcoming in *Le Genre humain*.

25. In his "Nouvelle lettre à M. Strauss" dated September 15, 1871 (vol. 1, pp. 449–462).

26. Friedrich Max Müller, whose work did as much as Renan's to popularize the idea of race, is less assertive than Renan as to the scientific status of this notion (see Chapter 5, n. 4).

27. On the connection between Aryan characteristics, mythological talent, and scientific creativity, see Renan, 1859, p. 434; vol. 7, pp. 339 and 737; vol. 8, pp. 149–150 and 1230. The inverse relation is just as obvious to Renan: "Semitic roots are dry, inorganic, absolutely unsuited for giving rise to a mythology" (vol. 6, p. 58).

The conviction that there was a correlation between the polytheistic spirit, generally Aryan, and scientific capacity was widely held at the time. Among many possible examples, see L.-E. Burnouf, *Essai sur le Véda* (Paris, 1863), pp. 464–469, and *La science des religions* (1870) (Paris, 1876), pp. 310–311; J. Réville, *Revue de l'histoire des religions* 26:2 (1892):85.

28. Bonald saw Judaism as a "religion of childhood," whereas Christianity was a "religion of the age of virility": *Recherches philosophiques*, p. 473.

29. A commonplace of early twentieth-century thought, this idea, along with that of the Hebrews' lack of creative power, can be found, but in a different context and with a different meaning, in a letter from Sigmund Freud to Arnold Zweig dated May 8, 1932: "To think that this strip of our native earth is associated with no other progress, no discovery or invention . . . but Palestine has produced nothing but religions, sacred frenzies, presumptuous attempts to conquer the outer world of appearances by the inner world of wishful thinking." *Letters of Sigmund Freud*, trans. T. and J. Stern (New York: Basic Books, 1960), p. 411.

30. In 1799 the Berlin pastor Friedrich Schleiermacher (1768–1834) praised the creative imagination as what was noblest and most original in human beings ("das höchste und ursprünglichste im Menschen"): *Uber die Religion: Reden an die Gebildeten unter ihren Verächtern* (1799), ed. H. Leisegang (Leipzig, 1924), p. 106. This belief was one of the central tenets of Romanticism. See H. Eichner, "The Rise of Modern Science and the Genesis of Romanticism," *PMLA* 97:1 (1982):17ff.

31. In the first book of his *Histoire du peuple d'Israël* (1887), under the influence of Albert Réville (1826–1906), whose *Religions des peuples non civilisés* (Paris, 1883) he cites, Renan tempered his claims concerning the primitive monotheism of the Semites (vol. 6, pp. 48ff). Once again, however, this was a concession without conviction. Renan's dogmatic blindness, his refusal to recognize ancient Semitic polytheism, is all the more significant in that he was the editor of the *Corpus inscriptionum semiticarum*, which abounds with epigraphic evidence for the phenomenon. J. Darmesteter wrote: "Without dwelling on what is dubious and dangerous in the identification of

the concept of race with the concept of language, progress in Semitic epigraphy since 1845 has revealed that monotheism was exceptional among the Semites. . . . The very *Corpus* founded by M. Renan has yielded countless relics of early Semitic polytheism from ancient Carthage, Phoenicia, and pre-Islamic Arabia. . . . These theories . . . dominate throughout all of M. Renan's work." From the "Rapport annuel" of the *Journal asiatique*, 1893, p. 57. For the constitution of the *Corpus,* which Renan proposed to the Académie des Inscriptions et Belles-Lettres on January 25, 1867, and whose the first volume was published in 1881, see ibid., pp. 74ff, and M. Vernes, "Ernest Renan," *Revue internationale de l'enseignement* 24 (1892):387–395.

32. Edgar Quinet, "Le mahométisme" (1845), in *Le Christianisme et la Révolution française* (Paris, 1984), pp. 117–136. Renan saw Islam as the most reactionary of the three monotheistic religions (1859, p. 422) and as the very expression of the Semitic spirit (p. 254). For the specific position of Hebrew vis-à-vis Arabic, see, for example, vol. 8, pp. 96 and 514. On the subject of Islam, apart from his famous lecture on "L'islamisme et la science," as well as the ensuing controversy with Jamal al-din al-Afghani in the spring of 1883 (vol. 1, pp. 945–965), Renan was often extraordinarily vehement. One example will suffice. Psichari quotes a note that Renan recorded during his mission to Phoenicia in 1860–61 in one of the black leather notebooks now at the Bibliothèque Nationale: "I, the most moderate of men, who blames himself for not hating evil enough, for indulging it—I am without pity for Islam. I wish Islamism an ignominious death. I would like to slap it down. Yes, the East must be Christianized, for the benefit not of the Christians of the East but of the Christians of the West": *Renan d'après lui-même,* pp. 213–214.

33. Quinet, "Le mahométisme," p. 119.

34. "Moderate" because less exclusively and strictly monotheistic: Renan, 1859, pp. 250–252 and 422; vol. 4, p. 125.

35. Quoted in Psichari, *Renan d'après lui-même,* p. 276.

36. P. Alfaric, *Les manuscrits de la "Vie de Jésus" d'Ernest Renan* (Paris, 1939), pp. 61–62 and 26. The first sentence is from the third notebook (Nouv. Acq. Franç., 11.483) and the second from the second notebook (11.484). Renan's family deposited his manuscripts in the

Bibliothèque Nationale in 1895 (Nouv. Acq. Franç., 11.436–
11.495). For information on the dating of the four notebooks in
which Renan took notes during his mission to Phoenicia in 1860–
61, in the course of which he visited Palestine, see Alfaric, *Les manuscrits,* pp. xvii–xix.

37. In his first notebook: see Alfaric, *Les manuscrits,* p. xxxi, n. 7.

38. In this discussion of the historical geography of Paradise, Renan,
    like J. C. Adeling (1732–1806), locates Paradise in Kashmir; see
    G. J. Metcalf, "Adelung Discovers the Languages of Asia," *Histoire,
    Epistémologie, Language* 6:2 (1984):107. Herder located the Eden of
    Genesis in India: *Ideen zur Philosophie der Geschichte der Menschheit,*
    ed. B. Suphan, vol. 13, pp. 431–432.

39. Richard Wagner and Franz Liszt, *Correspondance (1841–1882)*
    (Paris, 1943), p. 327. Huston Stewart Chamberlain (1885–1927),
    Grundlagen des neunzehnten Jahrhunderts (1898), 2nd ed. (Munich,
    1900), vol. 1, pp. 189ff, considers the Aryanization of Christianity,
    which gave currency to an Aryan Jesus who aroused the enthusiasm
    of Wagner and his friends at Bayreuth. See W. Schüler, *Der Bay-
    reuther Kreis von seiner Entstehung bis zum Ausgang der Wilhelminischen
    Aera: Wagnerkult und Kulterreform im Geiste völkischer Weltanschauung*
    (Münster, 1971), pp. 275–276.

40. For example, L.-E. Burnouf, *La science des religions* (1870; Paris,
    1876), tries to show that "Christianity is a wholly Aryan doctrine,
    which, as religion, has almost nothing in common with Judaism"
    (p. 120). He also says that it is "in the hymns of the Veda and not
    in the Bible that we must look for the original source of our reli-
    gion" (p. 217). But Voltaire, a century earlier, wrote to Frederick
    II, the king of Prussia, on December 21, 1775: "It seemed obvious
    to me that our holy Christian religion was based solely on the an-
    cient religion of Brahma." See T. Besterman, ed., *Voltaire's Corre-
    spondence* (Geneva, 1964), vol. 92, letter 18677, p. 182. For a bib-
    liography of sources concerning the proposed Buddhist origins of
    Christianity, see H. Pinard de La Boullaye, *L'etude comparée des reli-
    gions: essai critique* (Paris, 1922), vol. 1, pp. 465–466.

41. In notebooks of preparatory sketches for the *Vie de Jésus,* in Alfaric,
    Les manuscrits, p. 16. See pp. 13–14, 16, 19–26, 31, where Renan
    contrasts Galilee with Judea, Christianity with Judaism.

42. On Renan's attitudes toward ancient Greece—intense interest combined with aloofness—see Pierre Vidal-Naquet, "Renan et le miracle grec," forthcoming in the proceedings of the colloquium "Le miracle grec," University of Nice, May 1989.

43. For a good illustration of this, see the second notebook, in Alfaric, *Les manuscrits,* pp. 20–21. Burnouf, *La science,* goes so far as to see "two races" in the Jewish people: one Semite, which gave rise to "the bulk of the people of Israel," the other, "the minority," "probably Aryas," who settled "to the north of Jerusalem, in Galilee," and who "resembled Poles." He argues that this Aryan Galilee was the birthplace of Christianity, which was rooted in Aryan Zoroastrianism (pp. 117 and 303).

44. During his mission to Phoenicia (1860–61), Renan spent a month in Palestine in the spring of 1861.

45. Alfaric, *Les manuscrits,* p. 13.

46. Psichari, *Renan d'après lui-même,* p. 196. Born on September 30, 1884, Euphrosyne Psichari, known as Henriette, was the second child of Noémi Renan (1862–1943) and Jean Psichari (1854–1929). She died in 1972 after completing publication of her grandfather's *Oeuvres complètes* by the publisher Calmann-Lévy, formerly Michel Lévy Frères.

47. From the second notebook, in Alfaric, *Les manuscrits,* pp. 21 and 26.

48. In *L'avenir de la science* Renan asserted: "Form and style are three-quarters of thought, and there is nothing wrong with that, despite the objections of certain puritans" (vol. 3, p. 850).

49. In addition to H. Psichari, *Renan d'après lui-même,* aspects of Renan's life may be gleaned from J. G. Frazer, *Sur Ernest Renan* (Paris, 1923); A. Réville, "Ernest Renan," *Revue de l'histoire des religions* 26:2 (1892):220–226; M. Vernes, "Ernest Renan," *Revue internationale de l'enseignement* 24 (1892):380, 386; J. Darmesteter, "Rapport annuel," *Journal asiatique* (1893):38; M. Vernes, "Ernest Renan et la question religieuse en France," *Revue de Belgique* (1899):28; A. Dupon-Sommer, "Ernest Renan et ses voyages," *Comptes rendus de l'Académie des inscriptions et belles-lettres des séances de l'année 1973* (Paris, 1974), p. 604.

50. Renan had read the *Ideas* in Quinet's translation (1827–28) and the *Poetry of the Hebrews* in that of Baroness A. de Carlowitz (1846).

51. Here I am relying on the "Explications à mes collègues" (vol. 1, pp. 143–172), published by Renan in 1862 after the suspension of his course at the Collège de France. His assertions regarding Christianity and the religious future of Europe are identical with those in previously cited texts such as "L'avenir religieux des sociétés modernes" (vol. 1, pp. 233–281), *La vie de Jésus, Histoire d'Israël,* and *Marc-Aurèle.*

52. For "Renan's position on Jesus," see the admirable text of H. Psichari, *Renan d'après lui-même,* pp. 215–219, which discusses the religious significance of the "son of God." In his notebooks (Alfaric, *Les manuscrits,* p. 4), Renan asked: "What was a son of God in this period?" He was constantly fascinated by the grandeur "of a son's relation with his father" (p. 217). An orphan, Renan had lost his father at the age of five.

53. Concerning this sentence Michel de Certeau wrote: "'Pure love' can be recognized even in the 'free Christianity,' 'eternal and universal,' advocated by Renan." See Certeau, "Historicités mystiques," *Recherches de science religieuse* 73:3 (1985):337.

54. In *La vie de Jésus:* "One looks in vain for a theological proposition in the Gospel" (vol. 4, p. 364). And in the *Souvenirs,* concerning *La vie de Jésus:* "Belief in the eminent figure of Jesus, which is the soul of this book, had been my strength in my battle against theology. Jesus has really always been my master" (vol. 2, p. 876).

55. Renan was influenced by the thought of Nicholas Wiseman (1802–1865), whom he read while he was at Saint-Sulpice. Wiseman, archbishop of Westminister, was made cardinal in 1850. He was the author of *Twelve Lectures on the Connection between Science and Revealed Religion* (London, 1836), which was translated into French in 1837; Renan cites it frequently (vol. 8, pp. 46, 55, 57, 96, 211, 222, 538, and 559, for example). The connection between science and religion, the subject of the lectures, is discussed on pp. 19–22. The immobility of the Semitic languages comes up on pp. 65–67. Linguistic affinities as the only scientifically acceptable notion of race are discussed on pp. 154–159. The similarities and differences between Renan's and Wiseman's anthropological conceptions have been analyzed by J. Pommier, "Etudes de l'édition sur les Conférences de N. Wiseman," *Cahiers renaniens* 5 (1972):75–81.

56. M. Vernes, "Ernest Renan," *Revue internationale de l'enseignement* 24

(1892):403. Vernes, the first editor of the *Revue de l'histoire des religions* (founded 1880), taught "religions of the Semitic peoples" in the Fifth Section (Religious Sciences) of the Ecole Pratique des Hautes Etudes when it was founded in 1886.

57. G. Pflug, "Ernest Renan und die deutsche Philologie," in M. Bollack, H. Wismann, and T. Lindken, eds. *Philologie und Hermeneutik im 19. Jahrhundert / Philologie et Herméneutique au XIXe siècle* (Göttingen, 1983), pp. 160–161.

58. For Renan's analysis of the religious problem of the Third Republic in his *Marc-Aurèle,* see L. Rétat, "Renan entre Révolution et République: coïncidence ou malentendu?" *Commentaire* 39 (1987):592ff.

59. As far as imaginary filiations are concerned, Renan's identification became even more intense when he chose to compare the Bretons of his childhood to the ancient Hebrews, as well as when he compared, in a manuscript at the Bibliothèque Nationale (NAF 11.479, fol. 417–418), certain Talmudic legends with Breton folklore. See R. M. Galand, *L'âme celtique de Renan* (New Haven–Paris, 1959), pp. 52–53.

60. E. Havet (1813–1889), who taught Latin rhetoric at the Collège de France from 1854 to 1885, was the author of *Le christianisme et ses origines* (Paris, 1872–1884), 4 vols.

61. Y. Conry, "Le concept de 'développement,' modèle du discours renanien," *Etudes renaniennes* 29 (1976):27–32.

62. Ernest Renan, "L'exégèse biblique et l'esprit français," *Revue des Deux Mondes* 60:6 (1865):240.

63. See Chapter 2 for bibliographical information.

64. Arnold Van Gennep, "Nouvelles recherches sur l'histoire en France de la méthode ethnographique: Claude Guichard, Richard Simon, Claude Fleury," *Revue de l'histoire des religions* 82:2 (1920):150–158; M. Yardeni, "La vision des Juifs et du judaïsme dans l'oeuvre de Richard Simon," *Revue des études juives* 129:2–4 (1970):180–187.

65. Published in Paris in 1637 and in Venice in 1638. Richard Simon's first edition was published in Paris by Louis Billaine in 1674. On Leon of Modena, see *The Autobiography of a Seventeenth-Century Venetian Rabbi: Leon Modena's "Life of Judah,"* ed. M. R. Cohen, with essays by T. K. Rabb, H. E. Adelman, and Natalie Zemon Davis (Princeton, 1988).

66. Preface, section V of *Cérémonies* (Paris, 1674).
67. Yardeni, "La vision," pp. 192ff.
68. J. Le Brun, "Entre la *Perpétuité* et la *Demonstratio Evangelica*," *Leibniz à Paris (1672–1676)* (Wiesbaden, 1978), vol. 2, pp. 8–9.
69. J. Le Brun recently lectured on this subject at the University of Liège: "Critique biblique et esprit moderne à la fin du XVIIe siècle," *L'histoire aujourd'hui: nouveaux objets, nouvelles méthodes,* (Faculty of Philosophy and Letters of the University of Liège, 1989), pp. 11ff.

5. The Danger of Ambiguity

1. For Burnouf, see Chapter 4, n. 8. Several studies complement the bibliographic information on F. Max Müller in the entry by H. J. Klimkeit in Mircea Eliade, ed., *The Encyclopedia of Religion* (New York–London, 1987), vol. 10, pp. 153–154; R. M. Dorson, "The Eclipse of Solar Mythology," in T. A. Sebeok, ed. *Myth: A Symposium* (1955) (London–Bloomington, In., 1965), pp. 25–63; Marcel Detienne, "Mito e linguaggio: da Max Müller a Claude Lévi-Strauss," in Marcel Detienne, ed., *Il mito: guida storica e critica* (Rome-Bari, 1975), pp. 1–21; F. M. Turner, *The Greek Heritage in Victorian Britain* (New Haven–London, 1981), pp. 104–115; J. Leopold, "Friedrich Max Müller and the Question of Early Indo-Europeans (1847–1851)," *Etudes inter-ethniques* 7 (1984):21–32.

2. Entitled "Comparative Philology of the Indo-European Languages, in Its Bearing on the Early Civilisation of Mankind" (1849, 153 pp.). This text, still unpublished, can be consulted in the Archives of the Institut de France.

3. Renan contributed to the popularity of Max Müller's works by having his wife translate some of them: see Renan, *Correspondance,* vol. 10, pp. 214 and 225. These translations were published by Durand in 1859 and reprinted by G. Perrot, ed., *Essais sur la mythologie comparée* (Paris, 1872). For the reception of Max Müller's work in the literary world, and in particular of the work of one of his epigones, G. W. Cox (1827–1902), which Mallarmé adapted more than translated into French, see B. Marchal, *La religion de Mallarmé: poème, mythologie et religion* (Paris, 1988), pp. 144–146, 344–346, 359–360, 404–405, 451–453, 462–463, 471, and 552.

4. Renan, "Des services rendus aux sciences historiques par la philologie" (1878), vol. 8, pp. 1230–1231; Max Müller, "Inaugural Lecture: On the Results of the Science of Language. Delivered Before the Imperial University of Strassburg, the 23rd of May, 1872," in *Chips from a German Workshop,* vol. 3: *Essays on Language and Literature* (London-Bombay, 1898), p. 187. Meanwhile, both authors hoped that scientific progress would one day establish the concept of race on firmer foundations: Renan, vol. 3, pp. 722–723; Max Müller, "On the Classification of Mankind by Language or by Blood" (1891), in *Chips from a German Workshop,* vol. 1, pp. 232–233 and 241, and in the Strasburg lecture cited above, p. 187.

5. "Semitic Monotheism" was the title of the chapter in which Max Müller criticized Renan's 1859 paper in the *Journal asiatique.* A French translation was published in *Essais sur l'histoire des religions,* trans. G. Harris (Paris, 1872), pp. 464–514.

6. In 1899 Marcel Mauss (1873–1950) summed up the attacks from the "anthropological school" in "La mythologie comparée selon Max Müller," *Oeuvres,* ed. V. Karady (Paris, 1969), vol. 2, pp. 273–275.

7. *Essais sur l'histoire des religions,* pp. 478–479.

8. *Nouvelles leçons sur la science du langage* (1863), trans. G. Harris and G. Perrot (Paris, 1868), vol. 2, p. 161.

9. *Essais sur l'histoire des religions,* p. 495.

10. Max Müller, *Origine et développement de la religion étudiés à la lumière des religions de l'Inde* (1878), trans. J. Darmesteter (Paris, 1879), pp. 241ff.

11. Max Müller, *Nouvelles leçons,* vol. 2, p. 79.

12. Ibid., pp. 147–148. Starting from Francis Galton's reactions to Max Müller's theories of mythology, J. Schlanger reflects on articulate versus inarticulate thought in "Dire et connaître," in M. Meyer, ed., *De la métaphysique à la rhétorique* (Brussels, 1986), pp. 95–101.

13. *Nouvelles leçons,* vol. 2, p. 149.

14. For his book *La science de la religion,* trans. H. Dietz (Paris, 1873). On the "science of religion" in Max Müller, see K. R. Jankowsky, "F. Max Müller and the Development of Linguistic Science," *Historiographia linguistica* 6:3 (1979):346–347.

15. See, written in the year of his death, the "Lettre addressée par M. le Professeur Max Müller d'Oxford au président du Congrès interna-

tional d'histoire des religions réuni à Paris le 3 septembre 1900," in *Actes du Premier Congrès international d'histoire des religions* (Paris, 1901), pp. 33–35.

16. Max Müller, *Origine et Développement de la religion*, pp. 261, 255. See also Max Müller, *Three Lectures on the Vedanta Philosophy*, delivered at the Royal Institution in 1894 (London–New York, 1894), pp. 27–29.

17. Max Müller, *La science du langage* (1861), trans. G. Harris and G. Perrot (Paris, 1876), p. 12.

18. Jankowsky, "F. Max Müller and the Development of Linguistic Science," pp. 346–347.

19. Y. Conry, *L'introduction du darwinisme en France au XIXe siècle* (Paris, 1974), pp. 91–107; Max Müller is discussed on pp. 101–106.

20. Max Müller, *Essais sur l'histoire des religions*, pp. v–vii.

21. Max Müller, "La philosophie du langage d'après Darwin," published in five installments in *La Revue politique et littéraire*, 2nd series, vol. 5 (vol. 12 of the collection), 1873, July-December, pp. 244–253, 291–295, 340–347, 442–448, and 483–490.

22. Formed in 1865, the Société de Linguistique de Paris gained formal ministerial approval of its bylaws on March 8, 1866. Article 2 of these bylaws states: "The Society accepts no communication concerning either the origin of language or the creation of a universal language": *Bulletin de la Société de linguistique de Paris* 1 (1871):iii. See J. Vendryes, "Première société linguistique: la Société de linguistique de Paris," *Orbis* 4:1 (1955):7–21. But see also S. Auroux, "La première Société de linguistique—Paris 1837?" *Historiographia linguistica* 10:3 (1983):241–265. In "La philosophie du langage d'après Darwin," p. 443, Max Müller states: "Today we know that the number of roots is unlimited and that the number of essential roots in each language is roughly a thousand." On the use of the the notion of roots by A. Schleicher (1821–1868) and Max Müller, see C. Porset, "L'idée et la racine," *Revue des sciences humaines*, Lille III (volume devoted to the "Myth of the Origin of Languages," ed. J. C. Chevalier and A. Nicolas), pp. 185–204.

23. Max Müller,"La philosophie du langage d'après Darwin," p. 489. For the rest, pp. 341 and 343.

24. (1861), pp. 16ff. Max Müller was one of the many inheritors of Herder's theory of the origin of language: see E. Sapir, "Herder's

Ursprung der Sprache" (1905), *Historiographia linguistica* 2:3 (1984):387–388.

25. Max Müller, *La science du langage,* p. 19.

26. Ibid., pp. 23ff. On "comparative philology" as a synonym for the "science of language," as well as other questions raised in contemporary debate on the subject, see L. Adam, "Les classifications de la linguistique," *Revue de linguistique et de philologie comparée* 14 (1881), especially the second part, entitled "La linguistique est-elle une science naturelle ou une science historique?" pp. 373–395. On the state of French linguistics in the 1870s, see G. Bergounioux, "La science du langage en France de 1870 à 1885: du marché civil au marché étatique," *Langue française* 63 (1984), volume entitled "Vers une histoire sociale de la linguistique," ed. J. C. Chevalier and P. Encrevé, pp. 7–40.

27. "Les sciences de la nature et les sciences historiques: lettre à M. Marcellin Berthelot" (1863), vol. 1, p. 635. See also vol. 8, pp. 587–588.

28. Max Müller, *La science du langage,* p. 17.

29. Max Müller further points out that comparativism grew out of a secular use of "comparative theology," a field of study that Christianity was destined to exploit from the beginning in its struggle with Judaism (*La science de la religion,* p. 30). See also P. Borgeaud, "Le problème du comparatisme en histoire des religions," *Revue européenne des sciences sociales* 24:72 (1986):59–75.

30. Max Müller, *Essais sur l'histoire des religions,* p. 80.

31. Ibid., p. xxiv. Max Müller also cites a Hindu convert in support of the same idea.

32. "Lettre adressée par M. le Professeur Max Müller," p. 34. A. Réville, *Revue de l'histoire des religions* 24:2 (1891):104–105, points out that Max Müller's call for this "legitimate place" was not always well received by Christian academics.

33. Max Müller, *Essais sur l'histoire des religions,* p. xxv. In the *Dictionnaire des religions* (Paris: Presses Universitaires de France, 1984), the editor, Msgr. Paul Poupard, cites the Vatican II Ecumenical Council in his introduction concerning this same type of "relations between the Church and non-Christian religions" (p. v). In Y. Raguin's article "Christ et religion" one finds a reference to Christ's "place

apart" compared with the other "great founders of religion" (p. 286). For an analysis of this dictionary's "at once offensive and defensive strategy," see J. Le Brun, "Un 'Dictionnaire des religions'?" *Revue de synthèse* 115 (1984):343–351.

34. Max Müller, *Essais sur l'histoire des religions*, p. xxi.

35. Augustine, *Retractationum* 1.12.3, ed. P. Knöll (Vienna-Leipzig, 1902), p. 58: "Nam res ipsa, quae nunc Christiana religio nuncupatur, erat et apud antiquos nec defuit ab initio generis humani, quosque Christus ueniret in carne, unde uera religio, quae iam erat, coepit appellari Christiana." See Max Müller, *Essais sur l'histoire des religions*, pp. vii–viii and 80.

6. The Monotheism of the Aryas

1. Bopp used a paper published by Pictet in 1837 (see note 5). See M. Bréal's introduction to Franz Bopp, *Grammaire comparée des langues indo-européennes* (Paris, 1866), vol. 1, p. xlvii.

2. On Pictet's brief career at the University of Geneva, see C. Borgeaud, *Histoire de l'université de Genève: l'académie et l'université au XIXe siècle, 1814–1900* (Geneva, 1934), pp. 251–255 and pp. 120–124 of the *Annexes*. I thank Philippe Borgeaud and Marco Marcacci of the University of Geneva for providing biographical references concerning Pictet. All the biographical information comes from manuscripts in the Bibliothèque Publique et Universitaire (BPU) of Geneva. These sources were recently examined by J.-J. Langendorf, who cites from them abundantly in his introduction to the correspondence between G. H. Dufour and Pictet (which is essentially one-sided, few of Pictet's letters to Dufour having been preserved). See Langendorf, *"Aimez-moi comme je vous aime": 190 lettres de G. H. Dufour à A. Pictet* (Vienna, 1987). Hereafter the introduction to this volume (pp. 13–128) is cited by the name of its author, Langendorf.

3. Roger-Pol Droit, "Victor Cousin, la Bhagavad Gita et l'ombre de Hegel," *Purusartha* 11 (1988):175–195.

4. BPU, ms. fr. 4222, 52, 54 ("Letters from A. Pictet to His Family"), quoted in Langendorf, p. 29.

5. A. Pictet, *De l'affinité des langues celtiques avec le sanscrit* (Paris, 1837).

6. J. Grimm, "Uber die Marcellischen Formeln," *Philologische und historische Abhandlungen der Königlichen Akademie der Wissenschaften zu Berlin* (1855), pp. 51–68, text of a lecture delivered to the Academy of Berlin, April 30, 1855. Grimm expresses his debt to Pictet on p. 54.

7. With Liszt she had two daughters, one of whom, Cosima, became involved with Wagner in 1863 and married him seven years later.

8. Borgeaud, *Histoire,* pp. 254–255, discusses this romantic escapade. Two years after the event, Pictet published *Une course à Chamonix: conte fantastique* (Paris: Benjamin Duprat, 1838). See Langendorf, pp. 44–53.

9. Published in Turin by Antonio Pavesio.

10. Langendorf, a military historian, gives technical, political, and emotional details regarding this thirty-year-long passion for ballistics (pp. 60–125).

11. *Les origines indo-européennes ou les Aryas primitifs: essai de paléontologie linguistique* (Paris, 1877), 3 vols; 1st ed. in 2 vols., 1859 and 1863. I use the second edition.

12. Pictet wrote "Arian" rather than "Aryan" for the race and "Arya" rather than "Aryan" for the indvidual (see vol. 1, p. 9, n. 1). Here as elsewhere, I follow the author's spelling and terminology.

13. The Indo-Europeans are characterized as peaceful pastors in an unpublished paper by Friedrich Max Müller, "Comparative Philology of the Indo-European Languages, in its Bearing on the Early Civilisation of Mankind," manuscript in the Archives of the Institut de France, 1894, pp. 40 and 117–118.

14. Influenced by W. Schmidt, *Der Ursprung der Gottesidee* (Münster, 1912–1955), 12 vols., K. Prümm developed a notion of original monotheism similar to that of Pictet, whom he does not cite: "In the third millennium, at the earliest, the Indo-Germans became a people *(Volkwerdung).* Now, if we find an original monotheism *(Urmonotheismus)* in most Indo-Germans, traces of which are at first distinct and are still discernable in the Persians, in the seventh and sixth centuries B.C., [original monotheism] is an innovation, which certainly was not a creation of the prophet Zoroaster but based on a preexisting disposition, we can gauge how deeply rooted *(verwurzelt)* this form of religion must be in the traditions of humanity." K.

Prümm, *Religiongeschichtliches Handbuch für den Raum der altchristlichen Umwelt: Hellenistisch-römische Geistesströmungen und Kulte mit Beachtung des Eigenlebens der Provinzen* (1943; Rome: Päpstliches Bibelinstitut, 1954), p. 819.

15. S. Lévi, "Les origines d'une chaire: l'entrée du sanscrit au Collège de France," in *Le Collège de France (1530–1930)* (Paris, 1932), p. 332. See also C. Autran, *Mithra, Zoroastre et la préhistoire aryenne du christianisme* (Paris, 1935), and P. du Breuil, *Zarathoustra et la transfiguration du monde* (Paris, 1978). M. Boyce, in *Zoroastrians: Their Religious Beliefs and Practices* (London, 1979), identifies Zoroastrianism with the sources of the monotheistic revelation: "According to tradition Zoroaster was thirty, the time of ripe wisdom, when revelation finally came to him" (p. 19). His first chapter begins: "Zoroastrianism is the oldest of the revealed world-religions, and it has probably had more influence on mankind, directly and indirectly, than any other single faith" (p. 1). For a critique, see C. Herrenschmidt, "Il était une fois dans l'Est," in F. Schmidt, ed., *L'impensable polythéisme: études d'historiographie religieuse* (Paris, 1988), pp. 301–339. See also J. Kellens, "Caractères du mazdéisme antique," in Schmidt, *L'impensable polythéisme*, pp. 341–371, and J. Kellens, "Avesta," *Encylcopaedia iranica*, vol. 3, 1 (1987):35–44.

16. Quatrefages wrote Pictet: "I have just studied your magnificent work and cannot tell you how impressed I am by the results to which your method of analysis has led you. This truly is paleontology, and, as Cuvier did for animals, you have resurrected this primitive society in such a way as to enhance our knowledge of contemporary societies." This letter is quoted but not dated in Borgeaud, *Histoire,* p. 124 of the *Annexes*. See also Renan's letter to Berthelot in the same year that the second part of Pictet's work was published.

17. BPU, ms. fr. 4228, 101 ("Letters from Genevans and Swiss"), quoted by Langendorf, p. 57. Other details on the relations between the young Saussure and Pictet may be found in the "biographical and critical notes" provided by T. de Mauro in his edition of the *Cours de linguistique générale* (1910–1911) (Paris, 1972), pp. 322–324.

18. Under the head "Variétés" on April 17, 19, and 25, p. 2, col. 6, and p. 3, cols. 1 and 2.

19. April 17, p. 3, col. 1; April 19, p. 2, col. 6.
20. Ibid., p. 3, col. 1.
21. Ibid., p. 3, col. 2.
22. April 25, p. 2, col. 6; p. 3, col. 1.
23. Saussure, *Cours de linguistique générale,* pp. 304–306.
24. Among the countless variations on this theological theme, see G. W. F. Hegel, *Vorlesungen über die Philosophie der Religion, II: Die bestimmte Religion; 2, Die Religionen der geistigen Individualität,* in *Sämtliche Werke,* ed. G. Lasson (Leipzig, 1927), vol. 13, p. 88. Hegel is commenting here on the story of the Fall in Genesis, a story that the Jewish people "long allowed to sleep": "Lange Zeit ist sie brach gelegen und erst im Christentum sollte sie zu ihrer wahren Bedeutung gelangen" (p. 88).
25. See Chapter 4, n. 34.
26. A.-A. Cournot, *Traité de l'enchaînement des idées fondamentales dans les sciences et dans l'histoire* (1861; Paris, 1922). A mathematician and philosopher, Cournot was interested in chance, whose laws he tried to understand using the mathematics of probability.
27. P. 662; for chance and Providence, pp. 626–627.
28. Friedrich Max Müller, "La philosophie du langage d'après Darwin," *La Revue politique et littéraire,* 2nd ser., 5 (1873):245; vol. 12 of the collection.

7. Heavenly Nuptials

1. As in the other chapters, I use the author's terminology. On the term "Indo-German," see Chapter 1, n. 46.
2. For further information on Grau and his work, see C. W. von Kügelgen, *Rudolf Grau, ein akademischer Zeuge der lutherischen Kirche: eine kurze Schilderung seines Lebens und Wirkens* (Munich, 1894). For his doctorate of 1875, see p. 16.
3. Max Müller called on one as a witness (see Chapter 5, n. 31).
4. R. F. Grau, *Semiten und Indogermanen in ihrer Beziehung zu Religion und Wissenschaft: eine Apologie des Christenthums vom Standpunkte der Völkerpsychologie* (Stuttgart, 1867). The first edition was published in 1864. Page references in parentheses are to the second edition.

5. Grau uses this idea primarily in another book, *Ursprünge und Ziele unserer Kulturentwickelung* (Gütersloh, 1875), pp. 114ff.
6. Ibid., pp. 2, 9, and 126–127.
7. The same general ideas are found in Renan, whose position was far from Grau's: "Without the Semitic element, introduced by Christianity, something would have been missing from the foundations of our intellectual and moral culture" (*Oeuvres complètes*, vol. 7, p. 727); "Judaism provided the yeast that started the fermentation, that is all" (vol. 1, p. 240). See also vol. 5, p. 1142.
8. "The difficulty for the Indo-Germans, then, is this: that in all their relations to the world *(in allen Weltbeziehungen)* they know themselves to be independent of and superior to all other peoples, but in religion they are completely dependent, and indeed on a people that has accomplished next to nothing *(so gut wie nichts geleistet)* in other forms of intellectual activity" (p. 119). And Renan: "Races that lay claim to nobility and originality in all things felt wounded at being the vassals in religion of a despised family" (vol. 5, p. 1143). And: "Above all the Bible, that thoroughly Semitic book which became the universal reading matter of the West, is the great sign that points to the religious privilege of the Hebrew people and the providential decree that condemned our tender young West to become, in religion, the vassal of the children of Shem" (vol. 7, p. 727).
9. "Die Ehe zwischen Geiste und indogermanischer Natur ist eine im Himmel beschlossene" (p. 257).
10. Grau also uses the ancient formula "Japhetics" to refer to the Indo-Germans (see, for example, pp. 235 and 250).
11. Grau, *Ursprünge und Ziele*, p. 3. Grau often uses the term *Zivilisation* as a synonym for *Kultur*. On the distinction between these two notions in nineteenth-century Germany, see Jean Starobinski, "Le mot civilisation," *Le Temps de la réflexion* 4 (1983):42ff, and p. 13, n. 1, for bibliographic information.

8. Semites as Aryans

1. *Sichat-Jiczchak* ["The prayer of Isaac"]: *Abhandlung über Ursprung, Eintheilung und Zeit der Gebete,* "von I. G., Gymnasialschüler in Stuhlweiszenburg" (the German name of Goldziher's native town),

published by Johann Herz (Pest, 1862), 19 pages. I have not seen this text, which is mentioned in Heller's bibliography (see below, n. 8), p. 17.

2. A term of opprobrium among traditional Jews, who had not forgotten that Spinoza was excommunicated by the Synagogue of Amsterdam. See I. Goldziher, *Tagebuch,* ed. A. Scheiber (Leyden, 1978), p. 22.

3. On Leopold Zuns (1794–1886), founder of the "science of Judaism" that arose after 1810 and was first formally defined in 1822 in the *Zeitschrift für die Wissenschaft des Judentums,* see B. Dinur, "Wissenschaft des Judentums," *Encyclopaedia judaica,* vol. 16 (1971), cols. 570–584. See also D. Bourel, "La *Wissenschaft des Judentums* en France," *Revue de synthèse* 2 (1988):265ff.

4. In 1860 H. Steinthal and his brother-in-law Moritz Lazarus (1824–1903) founded the *Zeitschrift für Völkerpsychologie und Sprachwissenschaft* (1860–1886).

5. *Studien über Tanchüm Jerushalmi* (Leipzig, 1870), his inaugural dissertation, was devoted to a Jewish commentator on the Old Testament who wrote in Arabic in the thirteenth century.

6. On this point J.-J. Waardenburg wrote in 1963: "In my opinion it is no exaggeration to say that Goldziher created Islamology as a historical science in the full sense of the word": *L'Islam dans le miroir de l'Occident: comment quelques orientalistes occidentaux se sont penchés sur l'Islam et se sont formé une image de cette religion* (Paris–The Hague, 1969), p. 244.

7. On a mission for the Hungarian ministry of education, Goldziher visited Cairo, Syria, and Palestine (September 1873–April 1874). In Cairo he received an exceptional honor for a European: the robes worn by students at the al-Azhar mosque. He was also invited to become director of the Khedif's library, but declined. For further biographical and bibliographic information, see Louis Massignon, "Ignace Goldziher (1850–1921): notes sur sa vie, ses oeuvres et sa méthode," *Revue de l'histoire des religions* 86 (1922):61–72; B. Heller, *Bibliographie des oeuvres de Ignace Goldziher* (Paris, 1927); Waardenburg, *L'Islam dans le miroir de l'Occident;* R. Simon, *Ignac Goldziher: His Life and Scholarship as Reflected in his Works and Correspondence,* including a selection of letters between Goldziher and T. Nöldeke

(Leyden-Budapest, 1986), pp. 11–76; on the uses of Goldziher's work today, see ibid., pp. 103–104, 124–125, and 160.

8. I. Goldziher, *Der Mythos bei den Hebräern und seine geschichtliche Entwickelung: untersuchungen zur Mythologie und Religionswissensachft* (Leipzig, 1876). An English translation by Russel Martineau was published by Longmans Green in London the following year, with two additional essays by H. Steinthal (rept. 1882; New York: Cooper, 1967). I wish to thank Maurice Kriegel of the University of Haifa for bringing this book to my attention. Page references are to the 1876 edition.

9. One was defined in terms of the other. In the Aryan-Semitic debates of the nineteenth century, the Aryans were generally credited with talents for both myth and reason, with creative imagination in the arts and sciences, whereas the Semites were characterized as possessing an inexhaustible gift for religious invention.

10. In his preface Goldziher recalls the works of those who proceeded him down this innovative line of inquiry, in particular, for Hebrew mythology, H. Steinthal.

11. Friedrich Max Müller discussed both the meteorological and solar tendencies of the comparative mythology of his day in *Nouvelles leçons sur la science du langage* (1863; Paris, 1868), vol. 2, pp. 271ff.

12. Goldziher used both "Aryan" and "Indo-Germanic" to refer to the Indo-European field of research (see, for example, pp. viii and xvii).

13. Goldziher (p. xvi) cites F. W. J. von Schelling, *Introduction à la philosophie de la mythologie* (1856) and mentions that Max Müller also refers to this work.

14. Goldziher had read all this in A. Kuhn (p. 92).

15. "Eine besonder Rassenpsychologie aber gibt es nicht" (p. 46).

16. Ernest Renan, "Nouvelles considérations sur le caractère général des peuples sémitiques, en particulier sur leur tendance au monothéisme," *Journal asiatique* (1859):426. Goldziher, p. 10, quotes Max Müller's "Semitic Monotheism" in English.

17. Contrary to Max Müller, who saw an "earthling" in the name Adam (p. 255, n. 1).

18. The *geschichtliche Entwickelung* of the book's title.

19. "Ham is the father of Canaan," according to Genesis 9:18.

20. Goldziher points out that the Bible refers to God as both Elohim

and Yahweh. The second name, adopted by the prophets, is "the true name of the unique God," whereas Elohim is a generic name for the idea of God. On Yahvist and Elohist tendencies, see pp. 357ff.

21. David Hume, *Essays Literary Moral and Political* (London: Routledge, 1899), p. 516. Quoted by Goldziher, pp. 317–318; see his comments, p. 318, n. 1. On the change in direction initiated by Hume (1711–1776), see F. Schmidt, "Les polythéismes: dégénérescence ou progrès?" in Schmidt, *L'impensable polythéisme,* pp. 27ff.

22. A. Réville, "Les ancêtres des Européens d'après la science moderne," *Revue des Deux Mondes* 49 (1864):722. A former pastor and liberal Protestant, A. Réville taught history of religion at the Collège de France from 1880 to 1906.

23. Renan, vol. 8, p. 578.

24. For a brief historical survey of the deciphering of cuneiform writing, see J. Bottéro, *Mésopotamie: l'écriture, la raison et les dieux* (Paris, 1987), pp. 75ff. On G. Smith, see ibid., p. 38.

25. Renan died on October 2, 1892. Concerning the preparation of this memorial address, see Goldziher, *Tagebuch,* pp. 153, 159, 165–166. The title of Goldziher's memorial address was "Renan mint orientalista" ("Renan as Orientalist"). See *Discours mémoriaux relatifs aux membres défunts de l'Académie des sciences de Hongrie* 8:2 (1894):1–100. Thomas Gergely of the Free University of Brussels kindly translated the quoted passages from Hungarian to French. References to this text are indicated by "Memorial"; otherwise unidentified page references are to *La mythologie des Hébreux* (1876).

26. A few months earlier, on June 22, 1893, J. Darmesteter said in an address to the Asiatic Society: "Being synthetic in nature, this work is for that very reason dogmatic. For despite the appearance of skepticism and the somewehat vague character of many of his conclusions, it is surprising, when one has examined the work closely, to discover that it is inspired by certain absolute principles that were laid down in his first paper and that were sometimes in advance or excess of the pure scientific facts." See "Rapport annuel," devoted in part to Renan's work, in *Journal asiatique* (1893):52–53.

27. Inaugurating his work in *L'avenir de la science,* Renan dismissed this type of argument as "puritanical." In a journal entry made while preparing his memorial address (May 16, 1893), Goldziher alludes

to Renan's "inflated sentences" *(geschwollene Phrase)* and adds: "Sincere people do not make phrases, and phrases can in no way contradict truths." See *Tagebuch,* p. 159.

28. Darmesteter on Renan: "These simple, clear, imperious formulas have, as is well known, enjoyed great success. . . . They were too simple not to seduce the public and the popularizers, for they presented an admirably clear framework of ideas and a guiding thread through history. But they were also too simple to fit the facts, and the closer one looked at them, the more one had to shake one's head" (p. 57).

29. I. Goldziher, *Le dogme et la loi de l'islam: histoire du développement dogmatique et juridique de la religion musulmane* (1910), trans. F. Arin (Paris, 1920), p. 1. Goldziher was here drawing on the work of the Dutch historian of religion C. P. Tiele (1830–1902).

30. J.-J. Waardenburg quotes several written reminiscences of B. Heller, who knew Goldziher well. On Goldziher's religion he wrote: "The flame of his fervor was never extinguished by his criticism." See Waardenburg, *L'Islam dans le miroir de l'Occident,* p. 17.

31. Translated and quoted by Waardenburg, ibid., pp. 115, 116.

32. In the final entry in his journal, dated September 1, 1919, Goldziher retraces this period, "the unhappiest of my life." See *Tagebuch,* p. 313.

33. Named associate in 1876, then regular member in 1892, Goldziher became a director of the Hungarian Academy of Sciences in 1911.

34. M. Nordau's letter, dated May 12, 1920, and Goldziher's reply, dated May 30, are quoted in Simon, *Ignac Goldziher,* p. 60.

35. On the career of this rabbi's son who was also a scholar interested in the theory of degeneracy, see M. Ben-Horin, "Nordau, Max," *Encyclopaedia judaica,* vol. 12 (1971), cols. 1211–1214.

36. Quoted by Massignon, "Ignace Goldziher," pp. 71–72 and n. 5.

9. Secrets of the Forge

1. Contributions to these new sciences were made by not only the works but also the institutional positions of Max Müller, Renan, and, to a lesser extent, Pictet.

2. Theodor W. Adorno, *Essai sur Wagner* (1952), trans. H. Hildenbrand and A. Lindenberg (Paris, 1966), p. 178.

3. François Furet, *La Gauche et la Révolution française au milieu du XIXe siècle: Edgar Quinet et la question du jacobinisme, 1865–1870* (Paris, 1986), p. 20.

4. Ibid., p. 66. Wagner and his friends at Bayreuth were in a sense active "dechristianizers" who favored a return to a purified ideal of Christ: see W. Schüler, *Der Bayreuther Kreis von seiner Entstehung bis zum Ausgang der Wilhelminischen Ära: Wagnerkult und Kulterreform im Geiste völkischer Weltanschauung* (Münster, 1971), pp. 271ff. Thanks to Hubert and Hildegard Cancik for calling this book to my attention.

5. Sylvain Lévi, *La Grande Encyclopédie*, 1885–1902, vol. 4, p. 46, "Aryens II. Linguistique."

6. L. von Schroeder, *Die Vollendung des arischen Mysteriums in Bayreuth* (Munich, 1911), argues that Wagner's work embodies the most ancient myths in conjunction with a philosophy of eternal youth (p. 120). For Schröder Bayreuth represents the fulfillment of the Aryan myth (pp. 8, 207, 211ff). See also Schüler, *Der Bayreuther Kreis*, pp. 216–220.

7. See also Wagner's letter to Liszt, cited in Chapter 4, n. 39.

8. Richard Wagner, *Siegfried*, Zweiter Tag aus dem Bühnenfestspiel der *Ring des Nibelungen* (performed at the Festspielhaus of Bayreuth, August 16, 1876), II, 239.

9. Wotan, disguised to hide his divine nature, had twins by a mortal woman: Siegmund and Sieglinde. Siegfried was their child.

10. A. Satgé, "Les circuits du savoir," *L'Avant-Scène Opéra* 12 (1977):11–18.

11. Adorno, *Essai sur Wagner*, pp. 23ff.

12. The vicomte de Bonald had earlier recognized the theological need for a mediator. L. G. A. de Bonald, *Théorie du pouvoir politique et religieux dans la société civile, démontrée par le raisonnement et par l'histoire* (1796; Paris, 1854), vol. 2, pp. 97–114 ("Necessity of the Mediator").

Index